FATHERHOOD

THE TRUTH

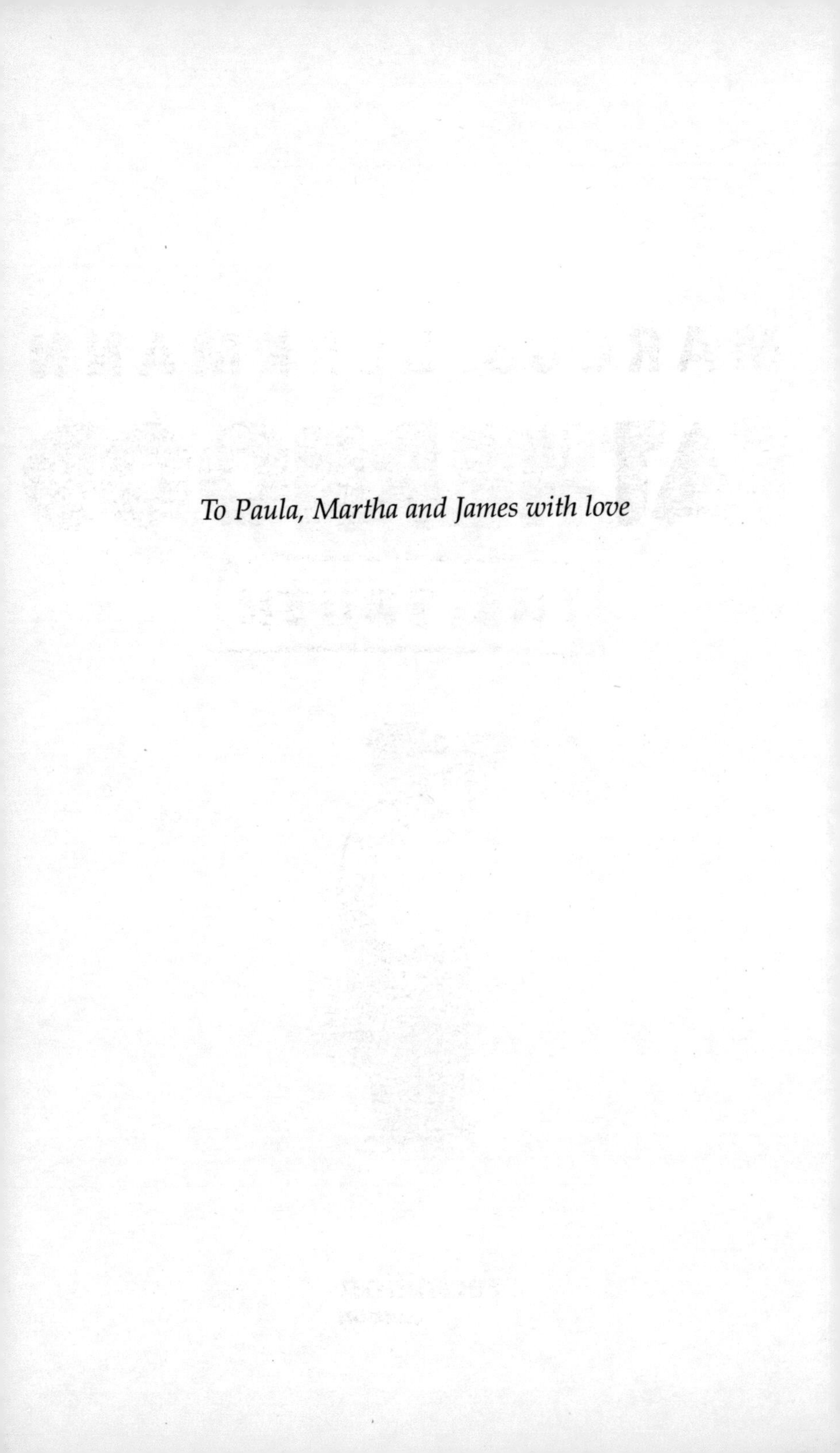

To Paula, Martha and James with love

MARCUS BERKMANN

FATHERHOOD

THE TRUTH

Vermilion
LONDON

11

This edition published in 2008 by Vermilion
First published in 2005 by Vermilion, an imprint of Ebury Publishing

A Random House Group Company

Copyright © Marcus Berkmann 2008

Marcus Berkmann has asserted his right to be identified as the author of this Work in accordance with the Copyright, Designs and Patents Act 1988

All rights reserved. No part of this publication may be reproduced, stored in a retrieval system, or transmitted in any form or by any means, electronic, mechanical, photocopying, recording or otherwise, without the prior permission of the copyright owner

The Random House Group Limited Reg. No. 954009

Addresses for companies within the Random House Group can be found at www.randomhouse.co.uk

A CIP catalogue record for this book is available from the British Library

The Random House Group Limited supports The Forest Stewardship Council (FSC), the leading international forest certification organisation. All our titles that are printed on Greenpeace approved FSC certified paper carry the FSC logo. Our paper procurement policy can be found at www.rbooks.co.uk/environment

Jacket illustration by Jason Ford
Designed and set by seagulls.net

Cartoon on page 4 by Alex Hazle
Clive Dunn *Dad's Army* image on page 127 courtesy of Kobal Collection

ISBN 9780091900632

The information in this book should not be treated as a substitute for qualified medical advice; always consult a qualified medical practitioner. Neither the author nor the publisher can be held responsible for any loss or claim arising out of the use or misuse of the suggestions made or the failure to take medical advice.

To buy books by your favourite authors and register for offers visit www.rbooks.co.uk

contents

foreword

I have written two books before this one: *Rain Men*, about village cricket, and *Brain Men*, about the sub-culture of quizzes. The first took six months to write, the second ten months. I wasn't a parent in those days. I would get up in the morning, start writing at about nine, keep going until lunch at about 2.30, do administrative tasks in the afternoon (washing up, shopping, 'quiz hour' on Channel 4), start work again at about five and carry on until my brain started to seize up. Every writer has a routine and this was mine. To say that I was engrossed with each project would be an understatement. Every sentence in both books was rewritten many times. I yearned for perfection, or at the very least, adequacy. Vast amounts of time were also swallowed up by anxiety, loss of confidence, staring out of the window and 'creative' mid-morning baths when inspiration had lapsed. I became incapable of thinking, or talking, about anything else. For six and ten months respectively, I must have been wearying company, although I was having a great time. There's nothing quite like extreme obsession for making you feel alive. In both cases, finishing the book left me feeling vaguely empty, and everyone else who knows me feeling hugely relieved.

When I started this book, by contrast, my daughter was coming up for three and my son had just been born, and a typical day looked like this: wake up at six feeling like death (boy has been feeding all night in our bed); summoned at 7.15 by girl who has slept beautifully all night and is now ready for the day; approximately two hours of childcare until partner gets out of bed; breakfast on the run; more childcare as partner, feeling even worse than I do, takes up long-term residency in bathroom and refuses to be budged; eventually start work at eleven, too tired to think; achieve nothing; give up as partner and children return from park/playgroup/shops for their lunch; more childcare, increasingly short temper, occasional 15-minute bursts of work, tears and recriminations, begin looking forward to bedtime; in early evening, bath, dinner, bed, stories, fights, arguments, desire to kill whole of family in cold blood now at its strongest; then, when boy and girl are finally tucked up in their beds, trip to off-licence to buy drink. Come back, start drinking. Occasional trips upstairs to rock boy back to sleep. Then more drinking. Pass out.

I haven't had quite so much time to rewrite this one. And it's taken me a fuck of a lot longer than six months.

1
bang bang you're dad

It doesn't matter whether you do it half drunk or half sober. It doesn't matter who it's with, or what it means, or whether you intended to do it in the first place. All that matters is this irrefutable, non-negotiable, inescapable fact:

You only have to do it once to make a baby.

Think of this as you approach orgasm with a tender 'Urrggh!', or even a triumphant 'Aaarghhh!'. Think of what's going on down there, the extraordinary complexity of this simple act that will change your life forever, and start someone else's. Think back to school science lessons, and those gruesome diagrams of a human penis in cross-section ...

It has, of course, been designed for this purpose (writers in Sunday newspapers will sooner or later call it a 'design classic'). The penis has a rich blood supply from the internal pudendal artery. An erection comes about when the penis's cavernous spaces – a technical term, as it happens – are filled with this blood, and the veins compress to stop it draining away (I think we all know what this feels like). Meanwhile, the testes are gearing up for action. Sperm have been growing there for several days. They are as ready now as they will ever be. There are 300 to 400 million of them in every ejaculation. They are not large. Each one has two distinguishable parts, a head and a tail. The head of a sperm varies in shape for each animal species. In man, it's flattened and almond-shaped. Each one is never more than five microns long and three microns wide (there are 25,000 microns to every inch). Inside are the chromosomes, which carry some of the characteristics that define you: the colour of your hair, the shape of your nose, your knobbly knees. It might help, then, to imagine each sperm as a tiny swimming plankton-type thing that just happens to have your face.

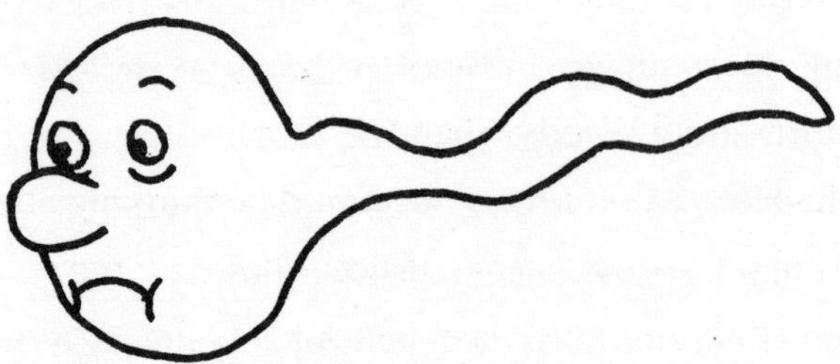

Fig. 1. Your sperm earlier today.

Covering the head of the sperm is a cap known as the acrosome. This is the bit that contains the chemical substances the sperm needs to enter an egg – the sperm's equivalent of a search warrant. You only need one sperm to fertilise each egg. He may be little, but my, is he potent.

So you cry 'Aaarghhh!' (or maybe 'Urrggh!') and the sperm start swimming. Their tails are about 50 microns long, and at the tip, barely half a micron wide. They whip and undulate, and the sperm move forward. Up the urethra, out of the glans and, because you have forgotten to use a condom, or have refused to use one, or have pretended to use one and whipped it away at the last minute (this requires practice and a plausible manner), straight into the waiting vagina and off on their long and almost certainly doomed quest.

Here we should pause a moment, as it's possible that you now have in your mind one of several images from Woody Allen's seminal film *Everything You Always Wanted To Know About Sex (But Were Afraid To Ask)*. Indeed, you might be unable to shake off the suspicion that your sperm have not your face but Woody Allen's. This would be terrible bad luck, as well as being unlikely. Each of the 400 million sperm in a good day's load will be slightly different. And chances are that all of them will be slightly different to Woody Allen.

No, the Hollywood films you should be thinking about tend to star Arnold Schwarzenegger, Bruce Willis or, if the video shop is about to close and all the best ones have already been taken out, Sylvester Stallone. Films starring these men tend to conform to certain narrative rules. Whatever Arnold, Bruce or Sly has to do to reach the end credits, the odds are against him. The chances of his reaching his goal are negligible. His enemies are many and powerful. All he has in his favour are determination, an enormous gun and a flak jacket/dirty vest/half-chewed cigar. But we know, and he knows, that Arnold, Bruce or Sly will make it to his destination or die trying. Not unlike 400,000,000 of your sperm, as they splash hopefully past the G-spot.

For you, as issuer of these sperm, the job is done. Indeed, you have already rolled over and started to snore. But the sperm swim, swim and swim some more. They can live in your partner's body for two or three days if they are lucky. Of the 400,000,000, approximately 24,177,489 will swim in the wrong direction and be disqualified. A further 156,436,002 will be eaten by ravening antibodies with sharp teeth, while 219,386,508 will eventually give up and have a lie-down. This leaves Arnold/Bruce/Sly and his lovable best mate who gets all the best lines but will be killed at the very last moment, just when you were hoping he'd pull through. These two will have swum from the vagina through the cervix, then a sharp left turn into the uterus and over to the fallopian tube, where a vast egg, or ovum, will be waiting.

Did she tell you she was ovulating? Did you ask?

But never mind about that now, for our two sperm are still swimming as hard as they can. And then, disaster. The Best Mate sperm is chewed up by an antibody. Arnold/Bruce/Sly is alone. Gritting his teeth, and firing his Uzi at any hormone that strays out of line, our hero makes straight for the egg. To him, it's huge – between 120 and 150 microns in diameter, slightly bigger than the width of a human hair – and full of chromosomes which, over succeeding months, will fight tooth and nail with Spermy's chromosomes for biological supremacy. That's for the future. For now, as Bruce/Arnie/Sly would say, there's an egg to fertilise. It swims ever closer, sure of its destiny, never pausing for a moment to wonder whether this is a good idea, until ...

POP!

Congratulations. You're going to be a father.

2

oh dear oh dear oh dear

So how do you feel? Now that you know you are going to be a father?

FATHER A (ANTHONY): Ecstatic. I'd wanted to be a dad for many years and it was like a dream come true.

FATHER B (BASIL): A combination of (a) elation, (b) denial, (c) an absurd and rather pathetic rush of masculine pride, and (d) a distinct sense that the world had changed.

FATHER C (CLIFF): Scared, I think, was the overriding feeling.

FATHER D (DUNCAN): Horrified, would be the answer. Surprised, shocked. It was unexpected, that's the thing. You've got

> *plans in your life and ideas and goals and things you want to do, and the news that it's suddenly going to change, it's a big shock. I found it quite difficult to take on board.*[1]

Myself, I felt my heart sink into my stomach, my stomach drop into my pants and my testicles fall through the floor. It's a strange sensation, being roughly half a storey lower in your spirits than in your body; and quite different, somehow, to other moments of crisis in your life. I have been sacked from jobs and I have been dumped by girlfriends, and both feel much the same. 'Of course,' you say when they give you the bad news, 'I totally understand,' even though you don't. You're just trying to maintain your dignity by being absurdly reasonable. It's quite different when you learn that you are going to be a father. 'I don't understand,' you say. But this time you do, totally.

It is God's little miracle. Or it is probability thwarted – the victory of blind chance against those very large numbers. Or it is a sign. Or it is simple good/bad luck (delete as appropriate). Some people try for years to do this. They work and work at it, wearing away their primary sexual organs until they are no use to anyone. Sex becomes a chore, parenthood an obsession. Many couples invest huge sums in IVF treatments, disregarding the ungenerous success rate, so desperate are they to hand on their genetic inheritance to another generation, whether that generation wants it or not.

---

1. The Fathers' Tales in this book are drawn from eight interviews and four written submissions. Each one is pseudonymous to inspire interviewees to ever greater indiscretions. Other names have been changed to protect the innocent.

It may have taken you this long, and this much effort, to make your baby. Or, to use Ben Elton's favourite noun (and verb), it may have required only a single, idle shag. It may have been planned, or accidental, or something of both.

Prospective mother: 'It's planned.'

Prospective father: 'It's an accident.'

(Note here for reluctant fathers. It is generally considered bad form to say 'It's a mistake.' It may well be a mistake, although few parents will say this for certain until their child is about 30. 'Accident' is more diplomatic, and less likely to be remembered later by hostile witnesses when everything goes wrong.)

But however it has come about, the result is the same. You are going to be a father. It's time to move to stage two of the process: Get Used To It.

THE ULTIMATE CHALLENGE

The books are very clear on this. Fatherhood is the ultimate challenge. By comparison, wrestling tigers with your bare hands is child's play. Scoring winning goals in FA Cup Finals? Any fool can do that. But creating something out of nothing, and then paying for its upkeep for a quarter of a century – that's a true test of your mettle.

Not that everyone thinks this. Some people (all of whom are women) believe that fathers have the easy option. Our contribution, they say, amounts to just a few minutes bumping and grinding (which shamefully ignores the several seconds of diligent foreplay we also bring to the feast). After that, they say, the woman has to do everything. She must lose her shape. She must buy a whole load of new clothes that are even less flattering than her old clothes. She must puff and gasp and swear as the baby grows ever fatter within her. For nine months she must feed this tiny succubus with the very core of her being. And then, when all hope is lost, she must endure the unspeakable physical and psychological trauma of giving birth. Whereas all we have to do is stand around looking faintly concerned.

They are right. It's all true. As is so often the man's lot, we must delegate much of the hands-on physical work to others, and content ourselves with a purely managerial or consultative role. It's our job, for example, to say 'Are you sure you should be carrying that? It looks terribly heavy,' while not lifting a finger to help. During their wife or girlfriend's pregnancy, if it hasn't happened before, most men will discover the Homer Simpson that lurks within. Look in the mirror: the process may already have begun. Women talk enough about the physical changes that they must experience during pregnancy, but men are not immune. You will grow fat, you may lose your hair, and beer will be your friend. And there is not the slightest thing you can do about it.

For while the women do the physical stuff, it's the men who must carry the burden of responsibility. Not economic responsibility, necessarily: I'm not suggesting that all men are, or should be, the sole breadwinners, although many will turn out to be. Nor moral, nor social, nor emotional, nor intellectual, nor political responsibility, come to that: each couple must make their own arrangements for these. No, I'm talking purely about internal responsibility – the weight of the knowledge that such a trivial event (unprotected sex) can have such far-reaching and long-lasting consequences. It is an extraordinary imbalance, and almost impossible to come to terms with. Women, luckily for them, are busy suffering the day-to-day misery of pregnancy. They haven't got time to think about any of this. Whereas, for the first few months, we have virtually nothing else to think about. And if you are at all reluctant, the same sentence will be going through your mind over and over and over again. How could I have been so fucking stupid?

You only have to do it once to make a baby. When do you learn the truth of this? Only, I believe, when you actually make someone pregnant. Until that moment you always assume you have a certain leeway. This may have something to do with the endless scare stories in the press about declining sperm counts. Thanks to stress, pollution, junk food and cheap red wine, British sperm counts are falling off the map. As a nation we are roughly half as fertile as we were during World War Two. By 2030, it has been predicted, a single man in Redhill, Surrey, will have to service the entire female population. All other men will be sitting miserably in pubs or having sex with farm animals. An entire nation will be shooting blanks. Eventually, randy Finns and Americans – the most potent nationalities, according to authoritative new research coming out of Finland and the USA – will have to be flown in to ease the problem. Resentful though we may be in our hearts, we will welcome these foreign usurpers, for without their assistance, our old age will be everybody's old age.

Bad news for Britain, then, but maybe very good news for British men who don't want to have children. If men's sperm counts have declined overall, chances are that each man's has declined specifically. Many of us, in other words, have been playing Russian roulette without any bullets at all. Who needs condoms? In fact, over-confidence breeds complacency, followed quickly by children. Sperm counts may be falling, but not fast enough to save you. Here are some good words to remember:

- fertile
- potent
- fruitful
- firing on all cylinders

Your testicles, which may now develop a psychosomatic ache, forcing you to take several days off work, are doing only what nature intended them to do. Good grief, if you felt like it, you could probably make some more.

Let's face it: man is genetically programmed to procreate. Centuries of civilisation may have eroded his ability to catch fish with his bare teeth, but he still wants to spread his seed on a Friday night. As adults and (we'd like to think) sensible, civilised human beings, we are naturally quite embarrassed by these compulsions and try our utmost to suppress them. Then we have a drink or two and make total fools of ourselves. All we are doing when we leer at girls is following our biological imperative, which is to impregnate as many of them as we can get away with. Kingsley Amis, after his sex drive faded away, said it had been like 50 years 'chained to an idiot'. It is this idiot who makes the babies; it is us who must answer for his actions. If this doesn't seem a particularly good deal, that's because it isn't.

In other words: it isn't your fault. Don't beat yourself up about it. All your instincts – which is to say your penis, and particularly the very tip of the penis when it thinks sex is in the offing – have been telling you to make babies. Your brain cells have been trying to tell you to have a cold bath and an early night with a nice cup of cocoa, but you haven't been listening. No one ever does, and that's just the way it is. Without men like you, selflessly sacrificing their youth and sanity, Britain would grind to a halt. You never know: it could be you in 2030 in Redhill, Surrey, servicing the entire female population. Then you'd be sorry. Or at least, very very tired.

3
the big questions

Once pregnancy is established, people will insist on asking the Big Questions. Some of these Big Questions have no answers. Some have too many answers. Some you will be asking yourself for the rest of your life. This chapter seeks to solve your more immediate philosophical and metaphysical conundrums, while shamelessly delaying the more complicated ones until later.

IS IT YOURS?

Well, is it? Here's a story to consider.

During the American Civil War, at the Battle of Raymond in Mississippi in 1863, a young soldier was hit by a bullet in the scrotum. Fortunately, it left as quickly and cleanly as it had arrived, but when next he looked, his left testicle had gone. Very shortly afterwards, in a nearby house, a 17-year-old girl was also hit by a bullet, in her case in the left side of the abdomen. 278 days later, she gave birth to a healthy 8lb boy, 'to the surprise of herself and the mortification of her parents and friends.' Three weeks later Dr T. G. Capers of Vicksburg operated on the baby, and extracted a miniball. Dr Capers had known the young testicle-deprived soldier, and came to the following startling conclusion: that this was the same miniball that had carried away the lost testicle, that it had penetrated the ovary of the girl and that some unusually hardy spermatozoa had managed to impregnate her. Boldly Dr Capers approached the young man and told him of his theory. The soldier, who obviously had nothing to lose (other than his other testicle), agreed to visit the young mother. They became friends, fell in love, got married and had three more children. None of these resembled the father as strongly as the first.

Oh yes, it's yours all right. Next Question.

IS IT A BOY OR A GIRL?

Heinz had 57 varieties; babies, fortunately, have only two. Everyone, though, has absurdly strong feelings about which of the two they want to have and which of the two they expect to arrive. As it happens, technology exists that can tell you for certain whether you are going to have a boy or a girl. At the first ultrasound scan (of which more later) the person with the white coat and the huge tube of jelly will know instantly, at a single glance. But he/she may not be able to tell you, the parent.

Unfortunately it has come to general notice that certain racial and/or religious sub-groupings in the UK are only interested in having boys, and would be inclined to have girl foetuses terminated without a further thought. Never mind that you may not be a member of any of these sub-groupings and that you wholeheartedly approve of the invention of the wheel. If it's hospital policy, and in cities it often is, the ultrasound person won't tell you. You'll just have to wait until the birth, like the couple with the seven daughters and the wild staring eyes who are next in the queue.

So forget technology. Instead, consult old wives' tales. You might as well. What they may lack in scientific methodology they make up for in sheer weirdness. All the following are guaranteed true – which is to say that some people genuinely believe them to be true, not that they have any bearing on real life whatsoever. And yet, who knows? Did these old wives know something we don't? Or was it the tales that were old, not the wives?

Let's say, then, that you too want a boy. Then, according to folk wisdom, you should have intercourse at night, or on odd days of the month, or standing up, or when there is a quarter moon. The prospective mother should sleep on the left hand side of the bed, and face northwards during intercourse. The prospective father should be the one to instigate sexual relations, and at all other times drink Coca-Cola. If you want a girl, both of you should eat fish and vegetables. You should have sex during a full moon, or during the afternoon. The prospective mother must instigate the sex. She should then make sure she reaches orgasm first, and after that she should think pink. You think I'm joking, don't you? In the United Arab Emirates there are only 52 women for every 100 men, and it's illegal to think in any shade between vermilion and aquamarine.

Even after conception, the old wives have some useful tricks. If an American woman wants to know the sex of her child, she is advised to pour Drano (a widely available bleach) down her toilet, and then pee on it. If the liquid turns blue, she'll have a boy. If it turns pink, she'll have a girl. Millions of Americans, possibly including Drano's marketing department, believe this to be true. Alternatively, a woman will have a boy if her belly gets hairy, or her nipples go dark, or her hands become dry and chapped, or she craves meats and cheeses. She will have a girl if she gets red highlights in her hair, or she craves sweets, or her feet get hot or her face goes spotty. Pregnant women who look a little rough around the edges will also have girls, because girls are said to steal their mothers' looks (you can just imagine the pursed-lipped American matron who dreamt that one up). Right breast larger than the left? It's a boy. Bad morning sickness early in the pregnancy? It's a girl. Brain feels as though it's about to explode? You've been reading too many old wives' tales.

And then try this one. Suspend a wedding ring held by a piece of thread over the palm of the pregnant woman. (Some versions of this insist that the wedding ring be the woman's own, and that the thread be a strand of the father's hair. But some don't.) If the ring now swings in an oval or circular motion, congratulations! you have a girl. And if the ring swings in a straight line, yes! it's a boy. And if the ring swings all over the place in no obvious pattern, you are standing out of doors in a high wind and really should take this more seriously.

Now for the Biggest Question Of All:

DO YOU ACTUALLY WANT IT?

Some men have wanted to be fathers for as long as they can remember. They have always seen themselves as fathers-to-be. They know what it all entails and they are prepared for it. They are lucky, lucky men.

> *ANTHONY: I hoped fatherhood would be the most exciting thing that had ever happened to me. It was something I had always wanted, but some of my previous partners hadn't wanted to be mums. It felt natural and the right time to do it. I couldn't think of a more worthwhile or satisfying thing to do or be.*
>
> *FATHER E (ERNIE): The overwhelming sensation I had when I first heard was relief. I'd wanted kids for years and years and years, and the big worry is that you're firing blanks. Second feelings were happiness, of course. Third feelings were, what does Eva think of it? I remember her being quite frightened, and then her deciding, if we're going to do it, let's do it properly. And then the fourth one was, I wonder if it's mine?*

A lot of men, though, are more ambivalent. There are no secrets here. You are among friends. You can be as viciously honest as you wish. If the answer is a big shiny Yes, we will be delighted for you. But if the answer is No, no one will blame you. And if there is a small kernel of No within the big shiny Yes, we will understand totally. You can say Yes! to your loved ones, you can scream YES!! from the rooftops, but look hard at yourself in the mirror and you might find that the word 'No' involuntarily pops into your mind. In some cases it's more like NO-NO-NO-NO-NO-NO-NO-NO-NO-NO, but the effect is broadly the same.

> *FATHER F (FERGUS): I felt depressed, in a way that I did when I left university. Knowing that I had to leave, when I had been very happy there, but knowing it was time to move on. Similarly, when the time came to have children, I felt depressed to have arrived at that stage in my life. And I also felt guilty that I wasn't more excited, and having to pretend I was.*

The brutal truth is that while most men would like children at some point, not every man wants them right now. It's not a good time. You've got work to think about. Money's too tight to mention. There are other things you'd rather be doing. You're too young. Life is fine as it is. You have problems with commitment. What about football on Saturdays? The flat's too small. You were going to split up with her soon anyway. You don't want to sell your nifty bachelor's car and buy a Volvo. Everyone has his reasons. They are all good reasons, and they are all the same. It's all a bit too much like hard work.

To which your partner will say something like: 'That's totally selfish'.

And what if it is?

You are a hunter-gatherer. It is your job to be selfish, when strangling a deer with your bare hands. And right now you would prefer to eat all that deer meat yourself, rather than having to give the best bits to young Jocasta or Kelly-Marie or Sid. (And isn't wanting to have children every bit as selfish as not wanting to? It is, but she will say that she is driven by fundamental biological needs, whereas you are just lazy and feckless. There is no winning this argument, although we all give it a go hundreds of times.)

Viewed from your current state of comfort (soon to end) there is no obvious upside to parenthood. Children are nasty, brutish and short. They are also expensive, malodorous and excessively fond of fish fingers. You have seen friends of yours, once young and vibrant, who within months of childbirth have been reduced to wizened, elderly husks, shorn of all hope and facing almost certain bankruptcy when the next credit card bill arrives. Years have passed: you have seen the men grow fat and complacent, the women become bitter and start eating Ryvita. Everyone shouts at each other all the time. Their sex life, so far as you can determine, has ceased. Having done what they were designed to do – create a screaming small child – their organs have withered and, in extreme cases, vanished completely. These are the people who now hang out in DIY shops, glumly eyeing up planks.

Before all this happened to me, I believed implicitly that people had children because it was the best way of filling up time. If you haven't time to do anything else or think of anything else, you are less likely to brood on the desperate pointlessness of human existence, and so leap to your death off the nearest bridge. Only by exhausting yourself into premature old age can you still these doubts and anxieties, for then even the most meagre treat becomes something to savour. At my local pub I used to see a father of two who had managed to escape for perhaps 45 minutes to enjoy a pint of bitter, which he consumed in silence with a manly tear in his eye. No one talked to him. No one wanted to disturb him. Sometimes he would finish his drink too quickly. You could see him wrestling with his conscience. Did he have time for another quick half? Could he afford it? He was a successful writer with a healthy and ever-expanding income, but you would never have guessed it by the way he peered pitifully at his handful of small change. Every extra sip, you felt, would tear a disposable nappy off his youngest son's freezing body. And so, head bowed, he trudged out, sighing like a corpse expelling its last breath of air. He wasn't the most glowing advertisement for the joys of fatherhood.

Selfish, lazy, feckless ... but then men are hard-wired to think mainly in the short term, to act now and think later and jut our jaws against everything the world throws at us. One such obstacle is womankind's often overwhelming need to make babies. Indeed, this may be mentioned as early as the first date. Imagine the scene. You are in a louche Italian restaurant. Things are going well. The waiters are friendly and helpful, and you have yet to spill a single drop of pasta sauce on your trousers. You slosh a little more red wine into her glass. You are talking about yourself. You haven't the faintest idea what is going to happen next. Life doesn't get any better than this.

And then, when you briefly stop talking to shovel in a bit of food, she pounces.

'Do you want children?'

First priority here is not to spit your mouthful of food halfway across the restaurant. But this also allows your brain to chug into action for the two seconds it needs to formulate the instant and appropriate lie.

'Oh yeah, definitely, yeah. I love children.'

No you don't. She looks you straight in the eye. She knows you are only saying this as a form of verbal foreplay, that you don't mean a syllable of it. She knows you are Short Term Man. But then so is everyone else. What is a girl to do? Simple. She will remember everything you have just said for later use, should the relationship get that far.

'Oh yeah, definitely, yeah. I love children.'

You may never be forgiven for this lie, however many times you apologise for it. Did you only want me for my sperm? you will ask, years afterwards. Well no, of course not, she will say (failing to look you straight in the eye), but you misled me, and we had only just met. Which is what any man would do, you will respond. For if we all said 'No, I detest children with a passion and wish to stove their tiny heads in with a mallet', then our chances of what might be called 'getting a result' would be sharply diminished. Only you probably won't say this last bit, but just tell another lie instead.

One problem is that most of us have only the haziest, vaguest notions of what it is going to be like. I asked the fathers what their preconceptions and expectations of fatherhood had been, how they imagined it would be.

FATHER G (GUY): Most of my preconceptions of fatherhood were influenced by memories of my own father. I suppose I thought you had to be rather grown-up to be a father. Because I remember my father as being rather grown-up. It seemed impossible. Thinking, oh my God, how am I going to be suddenly grown-up overnight – a serious person, who didn't have time for fripperies and banalities, just did serious stuff like mow the lawn and wash the car at the weekend. Smoke cigars, drink whisky. I didn't see how I was going to get to that. Fortunately I never had to.

FATHER H (HARVEY): I largely expected that I would take to smoking a pipe and spending more time in the shed making things from balsa wood. Neither has proved true.

FATHER I (IVAN): I reckon I thought the same as everyone else. If you have a boy you are spending endless days playing football in the park, and you are bringing up this little image of yourself. And if it's a girl you do nice girly things with them instead. The main thing I remember about my preconceptions is that they all turned out to be completely wrong. It's the classic phrase: it won't change our lives. Which we uttered more than once. We're not going to let it change our lives. There's no reason why we can't juggle work and motherhood and fatherhood and all the rest of it. Of course, it's complete bollocks.

FATHER J (JEROME): I don't think it ever occurred to me how it would pan out. Because I had no contact with small children, I had no idea of what they can give you back, or how much effort it was going to be. I suppose I had a vague idea of contented bliss, like everybody else, but being freelance I was worried all the time that work would dry up and that I would be desperate to get regular work, as I knew it would be financially demanding. I had no idea how *financially demanding. I mean, you just don't think. But my knowledge of children up to then came from going to weddings and seeing the best man's children running around your feet and knocking over the cake, and then hearing him wish the bride and groom the joy of children ... well, you just think, feed that child razorblades. I had no idea of what to expect at all. It was a big blank void waiting for me.*

Real fathers will tell us how satisfying it is, how fulfilling, and that they wouldn't be without their children. And we believe them. We also believe they have been brainwashed. They are the Stepford Fathers, rewarded for their loss of freedom with a new pair of slippers and some exciting new hairs growing out of their ears. Or maybe this is the parenthood equivalent of the Stockholm Effect, where hostages start to sympathise with their kidnappers. Or perhaps they just want to lure us all into the web they happen to be stuck in, so we can all be eaten by giant spiders together.

Barmy? Very possibly, but then I believe that a lot of men go slightly insane when faced with the prospect of imminent fatherhood. Some flee in panic, never to return. Others insist on an abortion, despite the terminal damage that might inflict on the relationship. A few propose marriage – which, on second thoughts, might be the perfect way of distracting your attention, for if you're too busy thinking about speeches and churches and guest lists, you won't be thinking too much of the vertiginous horror of becoming a Dad. Celebrate your loss of freedom in the most public way possible. Accept the end of youth with an enormous party that will cost someone - usually her furious parents - an absolute fortune.[2]

Do you want this baby? Maybe you do, maybe you don't, but in the end most men go along with it anyway. Call it an overwhelming sense of responsibility if you like, although dismal inertia may be nearer the mark. Coming to terms with impending fatherhood has much in common with the process of bereavement. First you feel anger (it's not mine, you bitch), then denial (whose is it then, you bitch?), then despair (oh fuck, oh fuck, my life is over), then bargaining (well you never know, it might not be too bad), then finally acceptance (will you marry me?). You have mourned your lost youth and freedoms before you have actually lost them, which may seem foolish but will save time later. Besides, once you are inured to what is happening, there is a far more dreadful prospect on the horizon.

It is time to tell your friends and loved ones.

---

2. According to British birth statistics, a first child is most likely to be born in the sixth month after marriage - and it has been that way for decades. Tell your parents this and see if they blush.

4

the first trimester

Reactions from assorted friends and loved ones.

1. 'HAHAHAHA! HAHAHAHA! You've got it all to come! You won't know what hit you! I've only just come out the other side! I've just been for a coffee with a friend of mine! Now I'm going home to do some gardening! I've got a whole hour free before I have to pick them up from school! HAHAHAHAHAHA!'
2. 'Oh darling, congratulations. You must be so happy. What wonderful news.' (Thinks: 'A grandchild at last.')
3. 'Congratulations. Well done. Hang on, I've got a call on the other line, got to go, talk to you soon, bye.' Click. Buzz.

4. 'I knew it. I said so last summer. I knew this would happen. I could feel it in my water. I'm a bit psychic, you know.'
5. 'Have you been to the doctor yet? Have you had your first scan? Chosen a hospital? Blood tests? Have you thought about a home birth? Any idea about names? Do you know the sex yet? Are you going to move house? Have you booked antenatal classes? They get booked up months in advance ...'
6. 'Two pieces of advice. Change a really shitty nappy very early on just to show her that you can do it. And make sure you change a nappy when your friends are round. They'll think you change them all the time.'
7. 'HAHAHAHAHAHA! No, stop it, I think I've cracked a rib! HAHAHAHAHAHA!'

Normally parents-to-be start letting people in on the secret after about three months. This is supposedly because it is much more common to have miscarriages in the first trimester, as I'm afraid you will start calling it[3], and no one likes to tempt fate. But the real reason is that it takes you that long to get over the initial shock and then pluck up the courage to say anything to anyone. Even if you are unambiguously delighted by the turn of events, it can be hugely stressful to cope with the unabashed joy of your relatives and friends. Why on earth are they so pleased? Everyone will want to shake your hand or slap your shoulder or

---

3. Pregnancy is officially divided into three 'trimesters', i.e. three periods of three months each. Use of the word trimester in normal conversation immediately identifies the speaker as a father, a father-to-be or someone who should get out more.

even give you a manly hug, having seen people do this in films. And you will smile bashfully and accept their congratulations with good grace, as you know you are obliged to. It's a situation that seems to bring out the rampant insincerity in everyone. They are delighted for you, which means they are really delighted for themselves (relatives) or they honestly couldn't give a monkeys (friends). After the first few occasions you will begin to wish you hadn't said a word. After all, no one *needs* to know, do they? And you'll have to go through it all again when the baby is born, so why not tell them then?

ERNIE: The first person I told was my mother. And she said, 'Oh no.' And I said, 'That's not quite what I was expecting.' And she said, 'Oh no, this is wonderful.' I said, 'I've just heard "Oh no," mother.'

I told my sister, who cried, but couldn't get any words out. And I said to my brother, 'I've got some news.' He said, 'You're not going to jail, are you?'

BASIL: The first people I told were my parents, and I had a sense that I was talking to them for the first time as an adult (not entirely easy with my mother). Then I told my colleagues at work. I was at once showered with delighted hugs and kisses from several intelligent and attractive young women, which is hard to describe as anything but jolly pleasant.

JEROME: My mother was quite shocked that I'd actually had sex. So her reaction was a little muted. She couldn't bear the thought. But my father was fantastic.

GUY: I can only remember telling other men, because Gina told the women. But the men generally fell into two camps. Either they were not fathers themselves, in which case it was like telling them that you had been posted to the Ukraine for 18 years, and you got this pitying look of bereavement in their eyes, as though they would never see you again. Or if they were fathers, it was like, 'Aha! Welcome to the Ukraine!'

DUNCAN: I didn't like having to tell people I was going to be a father. I felt constrained by it. Suddenly, from being in a relationship but otherwise a single guy living your life, to being a father ... You become labelled as something else: a parent, rather than a young man. I found that quite difficult. But I don't think people necessarily expected me to be thrilled by it, so I didn't feel that pressure. I think people realised it was a new thing, it was going to be a new experience, so therefore I would have to find my way through it. It wasn't necessarily going to be joyous news for me. And obviously Dinah was disappointed with that.

But it is worth telling people, and here's why. The more people congratulate you, the more delighted they seem to be by your news, the more you will enjoy being congratulated and delighting people and generally spreading sweetness and light. You might even begin to think that it isn't perhaps such bad news after all. Amazingly, the pleasure of others can help reconcile you to your own impending parenthood. (It works for the mother, too.) Soon you will find yourself looking forward to telling people, for it is in man's nature to show off. You may even begin to enhance the whole tale with creative little additions of your own. Within weeks the gravest calamity of your adult life will have been magically transformed into a really good anecdote.

Call it a coping strategy if you wish. But all fathers-to-be gild the lily in one direction or another. Which direction you go in is up to you. If you and your partner have been trying to make a baby for a while, this can be effortlessly transformed into a story of constant and unbridled sexual activity, of sore thighs, cramp and mysterious groin injuries, and of precisely timetabled shags to coincide with ovulation. You can portray yourself as the plucky sexual footsoldier, willing at a moment's notice to go over the top with your bayonet screwed on. Obviously you have no screaming need to make babies yourself, but you respect your partner's dedication to the cause, which shouldn't be mistaken for desperation, good Lord no. Not that there was anything wrong with your sperm, we should emphasise. It was just a case of anxiety, of trying too hard. And if it required endless sex to cure the problem, that's just the way it had to be. (Note: This is a sitcom scenario, and your male friends are unlikely to believe a word of it. But that doesn't mean they won't want to believe it, as they may be hoping it will happen to them some day. Lay it on thick. Limp a little if necessary.)

Option Two, which tends to be favoured by anyone who can do Roger Moore eyebrows, is the Single Fuck Scenario. Yes, it took only once. Normally we use seven forms of contraceptive, including a full all-over-body condom, and only ever touch each other on the elbows. But just this once we got a bit drunk and one thing led to another and bingo! she's pregnant. Pause for dramatic effect. Eyebrows. (Your friends won't believe a word of this one either, but they will notice the awed response you seem to get, and will be remembering everything you say to use it one day themselves.)

Most other options are variants on these. They include The Condom Split At The Crucial Moment; She'd Miscounted Her Days; She Said It Was Safe, The Cow; and We Like To Plan Everything Down To The Tiniest Detail And Before You Ask, We Already Know It's A Boy.

But whichever brand of lies you choose, these are good moments for expectant fathers. Mothers-to-be are said to 'glow' at various stages in a pregnancy (although they would be the first to admit that they look like shit on a stick at others). Fathers-to-be may enjoy a similar luminescent effect for completely different reasons. Relentless ego massage is good for the soul, and can persuade the most stubborn doubter that fatherhood may actually be worth doing. You never know, you might even be quite good at it. As you look in the mirror next morning, admiring the cut of your jib, just think about the magnificent genes you are passing on to your child. They are far too good to waste. He/she should be grateful that you are his/her Daddy and not some other wastrel or fat bloke. So what's the problem? Isn't it about time you grew up? Can parenthood really be that awful? And if it is, you can always leave.

Incidentally, that last sentence probably isn't one you should say out loud.

* * *

Miscarriage, of course, is possible. Around a third of all first pregnancies end this way. The real danger zone is between eleven and 13 weeks, after which you're almost in the clear (around three quarters of miscarriages occur in the first trimester). It's at best an unpleasant experience, at worst traumatic. It also may be a one-off. An embryo fails to develop as it should, so the body cuts its losses and expels it. For some women a miscarriage is a sort of training run. Next time she gets pregnant her body will be better prepared and should make a stronger baby. Some women will miscarry several times before going to full term, but in most cases the probabilities remain in their favour.

FERGUS: The first miscarriage I hadn't really felt anything much. For the second one we went in for the scan, and they were putting the thing over the stomach, and there was absolutely nothing there on the screen, so we said, where is it? And she said, I'm afraid it's gone. And I had a delayed reaction. I remember being with some friends two nights after and I suddenly felt unbelievably sad and I burst into tears, rather embarrassingly, in this restaurant. The intensity of my response seemed to come from nowhere.

IVAN: That was fairly ghastly, the whole miscarriage thing, that was horrible. I think when you go through a miscarriage, it's awful for the woman, and men tend not to know how to react. But it's just as hard for us. Everything is focused on the mother. And fathers just have to get on with things. I found that quite hard. But it was great when she became pregnant again, because the

> *last thing you want after a miscarriage is a huge gap. It's like falling off a bike and getting back on again. I know that's a crude allusion, but ...*

Early miscarriage may not cause her much physical pain, beyond period-like cramps, but her sense of loss may be overwhelming. Do not underestimate her need to grieve. (Or yours for that matter.) A later miscarriage – 13 to 24 weeks – may be more physically demanding, necessitating a sort of mini-labour to expel the foetus. This is not something either of you would easily forget. But do not be deterred. However appalling the experience, most women who miscarry will give birth to a healthy baby next time round. For there will be a next time round. It's remarkable how many reluctant fathers-to-be lose all trace of their former reluctance after a miscarriage. Perhaps they needed a trial run too.

Incidentally, be aware that miscarriage seems to involve some of the nastiest terms in the medical lexicon. Doctors occasionally refer to a miscarriage as a 'spontaneous abortion'. If the embryo has not developed properly it might be called a 'blighted ovum'. About a quarter of miscarriages in the second trimester are caused by the cervix getting ahead of itself and opening prematurely. This is called an 'incompetent cervix'. These are not terms anyone who has recently had a miscarriage needs to hear.

If all is going to plan, your beloved should now be showing the first physical symptoms of pregnancy. Some unscrupulous men keep a list of these on their person at all times.

● Morning sickness. Or more properly, 'morning' sickness, as most writers on the subject are keen to stress that feelings of nausea can arise at any time of day. Some women will barf copiously, others will just mope around feeling ghastly, while a few are spared morning sickness and so are hated by all other mothers-to-be. Don't try and claim you are suffering morning sickness yourself, especially if you had a drink or two the night before.

● Tiredness. They vomit in the morning, and in the evening they are knackered. They're really good fun, the first few months of pregnancy.

● Weak bladder. Most men under 35 are correctly proud of their extraordinary bladder capacity, for which they will pay in later life with regular nocturnal visits to the toilet. For women, this process begins during pregnancy. Even in the first few months they can barely look at a glass of water without wanting a pee. Try and wean them off diuretic drinks like tea and Coca Cola. Alternatively, carry a bucket.

● Breasts. They will become tender and may tingle a little. This is nothing to do with you, although you may as well take the credit. The veins on her breasts may also be more prominent, and her breasts may actually feel heavier – to you as well as to her. So if she starts talking about moving up a bra size, try to be sensitive, and don't make any jokes about eating all the pies.

- Smell. This is the real killer, especially for those unscrupulous men we were talking about earlier. One of the odder symptoms of pregnancy is a drastically enhanced sense of smell. She will know that the milk has gone off before you have opened the fridge door. My partner says she could smell someone smoking on the other side of the street, even if she was indoors with all the windows closed. There are sound biological reasons for this: smell helps mother and baby to bond immediately after the birth. After only a couple of days a mother may be able to identify her infant merely by its smell.

The main thing to remember is that she, too, is having to adjust to a new and very strange state of affairs. Think of what is happening to her body. Unfamiliar hormones are whooshing through her bloodstream. Soon she will start gaining weight – a terrifying prospect to most women who are not already generously upholstered. Meanwhile, at all times of day and night, alien words and phrases are popping unbidden into her mind. Stretch marks. Varicose veins. Mothercare. Without being told to by anyone, her body is gearing up for action. For the next nine months it will have one priority: to grow a baby. Everything else, including the mother's health and well-being, will come second. The conscious mind has no role to play in any of this, which may come as a shock to the conscious mind, which has had things very much its own way up to now. But the body was already programmed for this at birth, and has been ready since puberty. The mind is the passenger here; for once the vehicle is driving itself.

So no wonder she's exhausted. If the physiological

upheavals don't get her, the emotional ones will. In the second trimester, during the 'glow' or 'bloom', she will be full of energy – enough to retile the bathroom, or build that new wall in the back garden. But for now all she will want to do is lie on the sofa and eat biscuits. Be kind. Encourage her to put her feet up. Score brownie points now, while it's easy to. Above all, be patient. She needs to be looked after. Is there nobody else who can do it? Then you'll have to.

Just watch out for the tears. When she's not tired, she'll probably be crying. Old weepie films will set her off. Country music, the sight of babies in prams, nasty stories in the news, memories of childhood and/or dead relatives or friends ... to be honest, even an unfavourable weather forecast may open the floodgates. Double your tissue supply and try to remain calm, for this could be the most severe test of your relationship yet. It's bad enough when they cry when there's something wrong, but for many men the non-stop waterworks of the first trimester can prove challenging. If you have had a hard day, you may find yourself glugging the wine with ever-increasing abandon, leading to the first great Vicious Circle Of Pregnancy:

Mother-To-Be Cries Uncontrollably
Father-To-Be Drinks Uncontrollably
Mother-To-Be Expresses Concern At Father-To-Be's Drinking
Father-To-Be, Now Drunk, Shouts

Why should mother-to-be suddenly express concern at your drinking? Because she can't drink herself, of course. Neither can she smoke or take drugs. Her doctor will throw up his hands in horror if she so much as looks at a chunk of unpasteurised cheese. And if she spends too much time surfing the internet, she will read bloodcurdling reports ('US study links coffee and miscarriage') that will stop her doing everything else that is fun, too. Still, you have to be careful. Pregnancy is the most extraordinary upheaval. During pregnancy and birth, virtually every part of a woman's body undergoes some form of physiological change. She can have backaches, bleeding gums, piles and nosebleeds. She can suffer nausea, heartburn, stomach cramps, headaches, joint pain, indigestion and crippling tiredness, as well as insomnia. Her feet can swell up, her bones can go soft, her saliva can taste disgusting. Have I mentioned varicose veins? Or stretch marks? It's a great list, which contains more than a dozen excellent excuses not to have sex with you. And I bet she can think of a few more.

5
the bump

She can't drink, she can't smoke. Pregnancy experts can roll out endless lists of dos and don'ts, and their long misshapen fingers wag bonily at you should you ignore them. Given the strictness of the advice now on offer, it's amazing that any babies at all are born without two heads or a packet of Benson & Hedges in their top pocket. Here is a quick rundown of some of the restrictions your beloved will now be suffering. You can be sympathetic and understanding, or you can mock loudly – it's up to you.

● Folic acid, which is one of the vitamin B family. Everyone knows that pregnant women should take folic acid supplements (it reduces the risk of some birth defects, like spina bifida). Now, I read that they should ideally 'increase folic acid consumption' not just before conception, but three months before they stop contraception. Does anyone ever find this out in time? Or is this advice put in just to make you feel bad about yourself before you have even started?

- Physical fitness. All mothers-to-be are constantly bullied on their fitness levels. Paula Radcliffe would probably pass muster, but no one else ever does. Swim 50 lengths a day! Cut out lard from your diet! Eat bananas by the lorryload! Have a leg removed to keep your weight down! By the same token, though, pregnant women must 'avoid violent exercise'. No more rugby league, then, and she may add this to the list of excuses not to have sex with you.

- Passive smoking. OK, so she has given up smoking. It was a struggle, and she has only stabbed you twice in the three days since, but she has done it, and you are proud of her. Then you read somewhere that she must give up passive smoking as well. Eh? Should she go around with a fire extinguisher, just in case? Or never leave the house at all?

- Environmental factors. 'Before conceiving,' writes Dr Miriam Stoppard, 'make sure you avoid X-rays, hot saunas and pollutants such as dioxins and PCBs (found in many garden and household products).' Christ almighty! was my first thought when I read that. Only the previous week my girlfriend had had her leg X-rayed after she had slipped in a pool of weedkiller in some Turkish baths.

- Pâté. Don't eat this. Can cause liver damage in babies. Don't even smell it (smelling = passive eating).

- Unpasteurised cheese. Gives them listeria (do all French babies have listeria?).

- High temperatures. Can damage foetus if maintained for several days. Avoid illness, saunas, piping hot baths, the Kalahari desert.

- Cat. If you stroke it, baby gets toxoplasmosis. Instead, throw can of Whiskas at its head. Ten points for a direct hit.

- Drugs. No, sorry.

- Barbecued food. Store raw meat separately. Don't assume that if meat is charred on the outside it will be cooked properly on the inside. Wear a placard around your neck with the words 'I AM PREGNANT' written on it in marker pen and ring a large bell to make sure everyone knows you're coming.

- Herbal teas. Steer clear of cohosh, pennyroyal, and mugwort. You do already? Very wise.

- Seafood. Beware of sushi. Might have tapeworms! Beware of oysters. Full of bacteria! Beware of fish fingers. Taste like cardboard!

- Soft-boiled eggs. No. Salmonella. Also, may really be dinosaur eggs and could hatch and destroy world as we know it. (Salmonella slightly more likely.)

Above all:

- Avoid stress, say the experts. There is only one way to do this. Ignore all experts.

By contrast, the following are guaranteed safe and carry no risk at all of anything.

- Biscuits (max. two packets a day).
- Daytime TV (EXCEPT repeats of 'Bergerac').
- Arguments with loved one (non-violent).
- Unprotected sex (safer now than it will ever be).

So where is it, this baby? For all her other physical symptoms the mother-to-be won't yet be 'showing', as elderly female relatives would say. But it's not the baby's fault that it isn't big enough yet. At conception you would need a powerful microscope to see it. By two months it is the size (and indeed shape) of a broad bean. By three months it's as big as a squash ball. By four months it's a largish potato. By five months it's a TV remote control. That's good growing, by any standards.

Meanwhile, you continue to wonder whether it's a girl or a boy. Are you going to have a boy who will play football for England? Or are you going to have a girl who will play football for England? Curiously it's all down to you, the father. As habitués of pub quizzes know, you produce sperm with 23 chromosomes. Twenty-two of them need not concern us here. They regulate height, weight, colour of eyes and likelihood of playing football for England. It's the last chromosome, the sex chromosome, that makes the difference. An egg fertilised by a sperm with an X chromosome will grow up to be a girl. If it's a sperm with a Y chromosome it'll be a boy. And here's what else we know.

- Girl sperms are larger and slower than boy sperms. They won't reach the egg as quickly, but they are more likely to get there in the end. They have more staying power, and they live longer.

- So to increase your chances of having a girl, you should really have had sex around two or three days before ovulation. Only the girl sperms will have lasted long enough to fertilise that huge furious egg when it is finally let loose.

- But if you wanted a boy, you should ideally have had sex on the very day of ovulation. Those lithe and athletic boy sperms will have reached the egg first, while the lumpen, large-bottomed girl sperms lagged behind.

- And even that may not be an end to it. You, as sperm donor, can have influenced the odds even before you engaged in full-blooded sexual congress with your beloved. For if you have been in the habit of ejaculating frequently in the preceding weeks, as well as going blind, you will have markedly reduced the proportion of boy sperms in your semen. If you have fallen out of the habit of frequent ejaculation – and let's face it, who of us hasn't from time to time? – then boy sperms will have predominated. A father of four boys may look pleased with himself, but behind his smug grin lie desperation and bitterness. He may even walk with a stoop. Whereas a father of four girls is often very good at table football. This also explains why so many people you know had a daughter first and a son afterwards (including me.) Armed with this information, you can spend many happy hours speculating about your friends' sex lives, just as they are speculating about yours. In medieval Germany people believed that if you had sex when it was raining you'd have a girl, whereas if the sun was shining it would be a boy. Haven't we come far?

Personally, I was happy not to know. I suspect that if you do find out, your mind gets to work and you start imagining all sorts of rubbish, much of it recycled from your own appalling childhood. Will I like this baby? Will it like me? You can speculate all you want, but the fact remains that you have no idea who this little individual will be – and simply knowing whether it's a he or a she won't change this. Until the birth all you will have is the evidence of your eyes. And until your baby grows to the size of a potato in the fourth month, you won't even have that.

At three months there isn't really a bump as such: only a hint of the joys to come. Swimming around in amniotic fluid, Junior is just about fully formed. Fingers, toes, eyes, ears – they are all there. He or she also has a covering of fine hair. Muscles are beginning to develop. Prod the infant and it will wriggle. It's a long way from being born, but already it knows that it doesn't like being prodded. Personality already! Fingernails follow later.

Even without the bump, the mother-to-be will be starting to gain weight. This may be a painful experience for her, and a deeply tedious one for you, especially if you love her and don't care how much she weighs. Such is the malevolent, misogynist influence of the gay men who run the fashion industry[4] that most women now seem to equate even the smallest weight gain with moral failure. But there's no choice in the matter. Pregnant women put on extra pounds. It may be permanent, it may not. The situation is scarcely helped by the example of celebrity mums who, eleven minutes after giving birth, have already regained their fighting weight – thanks to careful diet, eight hours' exercise a day, a staff of 15 looking after the child and a quiet visit to a plastic surgeon to have the rest of the fat sucked out by giant Hoovers. Other celebrity mums, of course, choose to adopt because they are too vain to undergo the rigours of childbirth, or too skeletal to be able to conceive. (I also understand that if you have had a lot of plastic surgery, you are also at risk of 'splitting' in lots of strange places, and having large chunks of foam burst out of you as though you were an old sofa.[5])

As it happens, much of the fat a woman acquires during pregnancy can be burned off by breastfeeding. The body is

---

4. This subject should probably be filed under the heading 'Don't Get Me Started'.

5. Disappointingly, this is a complete lie.

hoarding for the future. As soon as the baby starts guzzling, the mother's extra pounds should swiftly fall away. Indeed, she could end up thinner than she started – as long as she keeps on breastfeeding the child up to and including its GCSEs.

But that's for later. Right now all the mother-to-be can see are the extra pounds on the scale. It may hit her badly. She may lose confidence in her appearance. She may start wondering aloud what to wear. 'None of my clothes fit me anymore,' she will say, two months before it's true. Again, it's up to you to make her feel better about herself. Be kind and understanding. Shower her with appropriate compliments. Tell her how sexy she looks. Tell her pregnancy suits her. Her skin is glowing. Her hair is glossy. Her breasts look amazing. Give her the soft soap. She won't believe a word of it, except the bit about the breasts, which you have been staring at for the past fortnight. The absolute priority is: avoid the jokes. One man I know, when his girlfriend started complaining about her 'child-bearing hips', suggested they were more like horse-bearing hips. Remarkably, they are no longer together, although I hear their foal is doing well.

The fact is, she probably will be looking better. In the second trimester comes the 'bloom'. Extra blood is being pumped to her skin, so her cheeks look rosier: she literally looks healthier. By four months the morning sickness should be over, so she feels better as well. Her energy has come back. Her hair is looking fuller and thicker, because one of the strange by-products of pregnancy is increased hair growth. And it's not just on her head, either. Soon she should have enough pubic hair to stuff a decent-sized cushion.

And so to the bump, which should finally emerge around now. (If you can't make it out from the general weight gain then she may really have eaten all the pies.) It's a glorious thing, the bump – a symbol of woman's fertility, of man's potency, and of future profit margins at Mothercare, Baby Gap and Toys R Us. You may start fondling the bump (if she will let you), feeling around for movement within, staring at it, telling everyone about it, marvelling at its great round weirdness. The revelation hits you: that Women Can Do This, and Men Can't. Not that you hadn't known this before, for you are not a dolt. But it is only now that the profound truth of it smacks you between the eyes. For some men this is a moment to cherish, and may be the point at which you start fancying all pregnant women something rotten. For you were right when you were soft-soaping her earlier: she does look good, and as the bump comes into its own she will look better and better. (Fancying pregnant women need not stop with childbirth. If you are lucky it will be with you for the rest of your life.)

Other men, by contrast, feel excluded. They are not even halfway through the pregnancy, which itself is just a brief preliminary phase in the long horror of parenthood – and already they seem to have been left behind. The bond between mother-to-be and baby-to-be is profound and unbreachable. These men look at the bump with suspicion. It mocks them silently. It knows it will be getting all the milk, and they won't.

Between these two extremes are multifarious shades of grey, because everyone reacts differently to the arrival of the bump. You may love the woman but hate the bump. You may hate the woman but love the bump. You may love them both (hooray!). You may have just packed your suitcase and arranged to have your name changed by deed poll. Anything is possible. Oddly enough, it has nothing to do with whether you thought you wanted children or not, but then, as must now be coming clear, your preconceptions have a nasty habit of being overtaken by events. What is certain is that men who are virulently anti-parenthood can be converted almost instantaneously into cooing devoted überdads. Do not underestimate the power of the bump. Accepting its influence, and realising that you now want to write one of those soppy newspaper columns about how great it is to be a dad, can be a humbling experience.

And as all the books say, you can never start bonding with your baby too early. It may only be the size of a fat hamster, but it will know when you are fondling the bump, just as it will know when mama is watching EastEnders (it will dance to the theme tune). Babies can hear sounds outside the womb from about five or six months. Talk to the blighter and it will come to recognise your voice (it can hear your gravelly male tones more clearly than its mother's squeakier range). Coo and make stupid noises, having ensured that there are no hidden tape-recorders or cameras recording it all for posterity. Massage the bump gently and, dare I say it, sensuously. You could use the inner tube of a toilet roll to listen to its heartbeat. There are hours of innocent fun to be had, and not-so-innocent fun, if you can talk her into it.

I asked the fathers how they had felt towards the bump.

IVAN: I loved the bump, I thought the bump was brilliant. You hear a lot of stories about men freaking out because their wives or partners were pregnant and feeling threatened by it. I didn't feel that at all. I thought it was absolutely wonderful. I thought it made Imogen incredibly attractive, that whole bloom of impending motherhood. I actually found it very, very sexy. What could be more natural, what could be more magical? And it was magical. And as it got bigger, and you got kicked in bed in the middle of the night by it ... it was great.

CLIFF: I'm not very keen on babies. No, let's start at the beginning. I'm very unkeen on pregnant women. It's almost a phobia. Like spiders. I remember, as a younger man, crossing the street to avoid pregnant women. So to be actually living with one was slightly scary. So I'm not sure I was wildly enthusiastic about being asked to put my ear to her stomach and seeing if I could hear things ...

I think I was scared of fatherhood, certainly of being a father of a baby. I didn't think I'd be able to cope very well. And, frankly, I was right.

ERNIE: I felt incredibly horny. In fact I still swear I knew she was pregnant before she did, because the whole sex thing was very, very different. Of course you can rationalise all that afterwards, but it felt different. Especially as Eva didn't get big at all ...

I was desperately interested in kicking, movement, the position it was in. Also a bit worried because Eva insisted on keeping her bellybutton ring in throughout. Because bellybuttons often invert during pregnancy. So I was always expecting it to pop out in a fairly dramatic fashion, and fly across the room. It never happened, to my chagrin.

GUY: I think I was reasonably well disposed to the bump. I don't remember feeling jealous at any stage, or anything like that. I think I was worried that I would have to do more during Gina's pregnancy. My strategy was to treat her as if absolutely nothing had changed, in the hope that she would continue as if absolutely nothing had changed, and therefore I wouldn't have to do any more than I previously had done. I just about got away with that. Fortunately Gina is quite robust, and she wasn't really inclined to be too self-indulgent about pregnancy, either. So I think we did, both of us, take the view, let's try and get on with life as much as normal, and luckily that was reasonably OK.

FERGUS: I found the bump creepy. Made me think of Alien. *I found it increasingly hard to contemplate even the idea of having sex. Completely put off it. Because it was like this thing was there, that it was sitting up there, waiting. You were just visualising where you were ... going, and there was this head up there, not far away. I didn't like it at all. I find pregnant women ugly, undoubtedly. Unless they're semi-clad and posing for* Pregnancy *magazine. Even then they're not great.*

6
the second trimester

And then there are the scans.

Fathers-to-be, in this relatively early stage of pregnancy, will normally know little about scans, other than (a) there will be some, and (b) they will be expected to be there. Anything else you probably don't want to know, because most scans don't give you good news, they just give you the absence of bad news. They exist to foretell trouble. Some people don't want trouble to be foretold, and they tend to avoid scans altogether. If you have a stronger objection to abortion than you have to birth defects, this is probably a wise course of action. Most parents-to-be, though, accept the usefulness of scans and so will be trooping along to the ultrasound department of their local hospital after twelve weeks or so. For some it will be the first scan of many. Indeed, a few will develop a real taste for the procedure and become scanaholics. The NHS doesn't seem to mind. So nervous is the medical profession of producing a baby that is less than 100 per cent perfect, that if there's even the slightest hint of a problem, they will suggest scans, scans and more scans.

It will also be your first encounter with the great medicalisation of birth. This is a much stranger and more surprising business than you may have imagined. After all, most of our received ideas about birth do involve doctors and nurses and machines that go bleep. In all films and TV series, birth lasts about a minute and a half and involves about two thirds of the hospital's staff. And yet, as you sit in the ultrasound waiting area with other anxious couples, it may occur to you that neither of you is actually ill. Even so, hospitals can undermine the most vigorous feelings of good health. As you wait, doctors stomp importantly through corridors, carrying files. Nurses ignore you. Receptionists make it clear that you are wasting their valuable time. Even the cleaning staff look at you askance. Like all patients, you are in their way. How much more efficiently they could run the place if it weren't for all these ill people sitting on chairs and taking up space. After a while you might even find yourself coughing quietly, as though showing symptoms of illness will get you seen more quickly. (You'll know about this if you have ever spent any time waiting to be treated in A&E. Everyone exaggerates the pain and/or discomfort of their injuries in order to see a doctor before they die of old age.)

Eventually you are called through. It might be ten minutes, it might be three quarters of an hour, but it'll certainly be long enough for you both to catch at least one of the airborne viruses that breed in the hospital's air-conditioning system. In a small darkened room, the ultrasound operator is waiting with her tube of jelly. 'Lie down here,' she says to your partner. 'Sit down there,' she says to you. There is something of the ritual dance in all this. Your partner lies on the couch. She pulls up her top to reveal the bump. You gasp involuntarily. You haven't seen her show it in public before. The ultrasound operator starts squeezing jelly all over the abdomen, then picks up her transducer, a hand-held device that measures high-frequency sound waves bouncing off the womb and the baby's body. It is wired up to a computer monitor which, gadget fans will be disappointed to learn, is only in black-and-white. (Three-dimensional ultrasound is on the way, but as I write it is still too expensive for routine use in NHS hospitals.) The ultrasound operator passes the transducer over the abdomen. Ping! Up there on the screen is a baby. Well, not exactly a baby, but a few squiggly lines that might conceivably be a baby if you had the visual imagination of Salvador Dalí. There, says the ultrasound operator. If you look carefully you can see its heart beating. And there's its head, and its spine and its little feet and hands ...

'Wow!' you say. 'Isn't that incredible?'

Hmm, you think. Is that all?

After the scan is over the ultrasound operator may offer you a picture. You say yes, because everyone does. It is printed out for you. You express amazement and wonder and awe at this extraordinary technology, which has been around since World War Two. Slightly more advanced technology would print out a picture of a baby that looked like a baby. This looks like the photocopy of a photocopy of an artist's impression of a stoat. Most parents-to-be will show this photo to friends, relatives and anyone who can't run away quick enough. Other than proving that the baby exists, an ultrasound photo only has one important function: to bring parents-to-be down to earth. Just as you didn't want to know when other people tried to show you their ultrasound photos, so no one else wants to know when you try and show them yours. File it away and forget about it, at least until the child is 16 and can be embarrassed in front of its friends.

This is all flim-flam, anyway. The ultrasound photo, the warm feeling of seeing your progeny's heart beat, the sneaky glances to try and work out whether it has a willy or not, are all just distractions from the main business at hand. The ultrasound, like all other scans and tests, is looking for abnormalities. All sorts of things can go wrong in pregnancy. Many can be identified early. The latest new test as I write is the nuchal scan, which you can have done at around ten or eleven weeks (i.e. just before the first main ultrasound scan). This measures the thickness of something called the nuchal pad in the baby's neck. If this pad is thicker than it should be, then there is a higher risk of chromosomal defect, which could mean Down's syndrome. If that's the case, you move on to the next test, the amniocentesis, which comes at around 15 weeks. For this, they withdraw a sample of the amniotic fluid that surrounds the foetus in the womb. They don't touch the baby, but the test does carry around a 1 in 200 risk of miscarriage. That's how risks become quantified in this game – 1 in 200, 1 in 100, 1 in 50, 1 in 10. As you go through each test, so the probabilities seem to grow, and you stop sleeping at night.

GUY: We had a nasty scare with our first daughter. The problems arose from doctors saying things off the cuff without realising how new parents latch onto them. So at her first scan the doctor said, 'Oh yes, her bladder seems rather full, it's possible her kidneys aren't functioning. You'd better come back for another scan.' So you spend two weeks thinking, Oh God, the kidneys aren't functioning. We went back for the second scan, and this time the doctor wrote on his notes, 'possible IUGR'. Only Gina knew what this was, as she was a professional researcher and had therefore looked into all this thoroughly. She was aware that this stood for 'inter-uterine growth retardation'. So we spent the next two weeks thinking, Oh no! Now we're giving birth to a midget. A midget with dodgy kidneys, more to the point. But she was fine, of course.

FATHER K (KARL): We had a nightmare one. The scanner looked at the screen and confidently announced that the foetus had a cyst on it, estimated at 18 centimetres. So we had a fantastic weekend worrying ourselves about that. Then we went back and found that she had misread something and it was 1.8 centimetres, and that actually it had since disappeared – it was a piece of fluff on the screen or something. So we were well chuffed about that. We'd spent the whole weekend thinking about surgical interventions. A weekend in hell.

The medical profession, for all their good intentions, may not be much help. The more they try to reassure you, the more terrified you will become. First-time parents who have fallen into scanning hell truly know the meaning of the word fear. And yet the probabilities involved are usually tiny. 1 in 200 – how much is that? Nothing. Even 1 in 3 means it's less likely to happen than not. But in scanning hell, a tiny chance of something happening always seems to be magnified into a raging certainty. The truth is that most pregnancies are uneventful and completely successful. Even if the probabilities begin to grow, chances are you will have a beautiful and healthy little baby (or at least, as beautiful as your genes will allow it to be). Take, as an example, Down's syndrome. The probabilities rise with the age of the mother, from 1 in 2,000 for a 20-year-old mother to a terrifying 1 in 12 for a 49-year-old. But how many 49-year-olds are having babies? Very few. It's at the very edge of the fertility graph, and yet eleven out of twelve babies conceived by a 49-year-old woman won't have Down's syndrome. I think those are pretty good odds. With screening now almost universal, abnormalities have become rarer than you might think. Only around five in every 10,000 births these days are Down's babies. The spina bifida rate is even lower.

Far more likely than an abnormality are twins. These will definitely show up on the first scan. Instead of one beating heart, two. Instead of two waggly legs, four. Instead of one willy, one. So it's a boy and a girl then. About 15 births in every 1,000 are multiple births, and the rate is rising – in 1975 it was about 10 in 1,000. Partly this is because of IVF treatments, which commonly plant three little embryos in the womb – and sometimes all three develop. A third of all multiple births are triplets or above, although quins and sextuplets are much rarer than they used to be – the fertility treatments that produced them regularly in the 1960s and 1970s are out of fashion now. Twins mean twice the expense, appalling parental exhaustion and, almost certainly, no more children, because if it has happened once, it may happen again. Watch the face of the man who has just been told by the ultrasound operator that it's twins. The flash of delight across his face registers the huge pride he feels in his own exceptional potency. After 0.0014 of a second this is replaced by gloom and terror, which may mark him permanently. It's not great for the mother, either. Giving birth to the little loves is bad enough. Then there's the breastfeeding, which is apparently like something out of Dante's *Inferno*.

Whether it's twins or not, whether it's good news or not, after the first ultrasound scan some fathers-to-be fall into a bit of a decline. This Post-Ultrasound Depression, or PUD, as doctors don't call it, is surprisingly common. It is characterised by a sudden realisation that your life is going to change utterly, and not necessarily in ways that you had planned. The general whooping and hollering that characterise life as a single man will soon be replaced by early nights and a detailed knowledge of estate cars. These are clichés, I know. They are also true. And this is usually when it all sinks in.

My working title for this book was 'Drinking For Two' – a phrase I myself used a lot at about this stage in the first pregnancy. Not that alcohol is the solution to everybody's problems. Some men turn to drugs, others work too hard, and one man I heard of who was having an affair with his secretary, sacked her, ended the affair, hired a new secretary and started an affair with her, all in the space of a fortnight. In many ways this could be defined as your first real midlife crisis – unless you've had one before, in which case it's your second.

What might help is a holiday, or some other equally pointless expenditure. Which is where the second main scan, at between 16 and 20 weeks, comes in. This is the dating scan, which will give you Junior's ETA. Dating is, of course, approximate – so approximate, in fact, that the due date is virtually the only day in the next seven months on which you can be certain the baby won't be born. Even so, it has a wonderful way of concentrating the mind. Now you know how much time you have left. If you are planning a holiday or fun of any description, this is the official cut-off point. (Incidentally, airlines won't allow pregnant women to sully their planes after the twenty-fifth week, in case they embarrass all the fat men in business class and give birth in the corridor.) So how about a nice little trip to, say ... Prague?

FATHER L (LESTER): Our son was born in the Czech Republic where we lived in the late nineties. It would be fair to say that the health service had not kept pace with other institutions in embracing the changes brought about by the Velvet Revolution of 1989. This was no bad thing in some respects. Medical treatment was still freely available to all, even us foreigners. But it also meant there was a lack of sentimentality about the style of treatment you received. And there was the distinct feeling that while all women were equal, some were more equal than others when it came to being pregnant. Add this to the Czech propensity for calling a spade a spade and a forceps a forceps, while laughing in the face of pain, and you have a recipe for a memorable pregnancy.

A few months down the pregnancy road Lilith had her latest check-up with the kindly but blunt doctor, whose idea of prenatal care was a regime of cold baths, long mountain hikes and eight pints of beer a day. Lilith returned distraught, having been rigorously informed that her blood test showed that she had a more than 80 per cent likelihood of carrying a Down's syndrome baby. We had to decide whether to have an amniocentesis.

At the time, central Prague had two maternity hospitals. Friends had had babies in both and recommended neither. We went to the nearest, a large late-nineteenth-century pile of terrifying aspect. There Lilith was whisked into a room for the amniocentesis, which I was allowed to witness. But I was not let into the ward where Lilith was put to recover as it was full of girls who had just had abortions. Just what Lilith needed when she was facing the same experience should the test results prove unfavourable.

These results took three weeks to arrive. There was no way they could be processed more quickly, we were told. We would just have to be patient. Unfortunately by this time we knew the sex of our child. Czech is an inflected language and during the scan before the amniocentesis the doctor had referred to our child using the masculine gender. This made the waiting worse. Our son had become suddenly real at the very moment when we were facing the prospect of losing him. The three weeks were a nightmare. Lilith, bravely optimistic, insisted on our arguing about names while I glumly gazed into beer glasses depressing and embarrassing anyone unfortunate enough to come near me. Thankfully at the end of the interminable wait the news was good. At last we could look forward to the birth of our son.

7
the run-in

As you will have noticed by now, the physical changes in pregnancy are extraordinary and far-reaching.

AFTER THREE MONTHS

Baby: fully-formed body, eyes moving, muscles growing, has fingers and toes.
Mother: gaining weight, morning sickness gradually disappearing, heart working hard, tired all the time, crying at bad films.
Father: bloated, paranoid, drinking too much, telling everyone he knows that he is going to take all his money out of the bank in used notes and fly to Bolivia.

AFTER SIX MONTHS

Baby: can hear everything that is going on, muscles have developed but body is still thin, lungs now growing.
Mother: eating for two, appalling indigestion, either wants sex all the time or not at all, feeling the baby move, may be suffering from cramp, still crying at bad films.
Father: increasingly bald, knee joints swelling, staring at girls on public transport, concentration destroyed, liver now the size and constituency of a breezeblock.

AFTER EIGHT AND A HALF MONTHS

Baby: weighs six or seven pounds and is just over a foot long, lying in two pints of amniotic fluid, fat and healthy, raring to go.
Mother: huge, exhausted, tearful, furious, unable to find comfortable position to sleep or sit or do anything, blames it all on you, talking on phone to friends and relatives all the time and going quiet when you come in the room.
Father: has taken all his money out of bank in used notes in preparation for flight to Bolivia but left it on public transport while drunkenly staring at girls. Resigned to fate.

To alleviate the stress, or make it much, much worse, you might as well go to some antenatal classes.

It's not known whether prehistoric man went to antenatal classes. Certainly the Ancient Greeks opted out, while the Ancient Romans were able to plead a prior engagement. Throughout the long majestic sweep of British history men have somehow managed to avoid anything remotely resembling an antenatal class – until the last 20 years, that is, when suddenly antenatal classes have come to occupy every Tuesday evening, or Wednesday evening, or any other evening on which you usually do something more interesting.

And we play along with it because we feel we have to, because, let's face it, we are the first generation of men in the long majestic sweep of British history for whom it is compulsory to attend the birth (in 1970 about 21 per cent of fathers attended the birth. In 1980 it was 42 per cent. Now, according to the National Childbirth Trust, it is 96 per cent). So we might as well find out what's going to happen, whether we want to or not.

Antenatal classes come in a huge variety of shapes and sizes, as do antenatal class teachers. For prospective parents the problem is ignorance, a terrible void that needs filling now, or sooner if possible. Those who teach antenatal classes present themselves and their knowledge as the solution. They may have been through the experience themselves, or they may have presided over it many times, but one thing always applies: they will think they know what's best for you. It's a rare antenatal class teacher who approaches the task without at least a soupçon of evangelical fervour. You want the answers, and you will get them. What you may not realise is that if you went to a different class you would probably get completely different answers. If you go to too many antenatal classes, as I fear I did, you end up with so many mutually contradictory answers you don't know what's what.

The issues at stake are how you want to have this baby, and

how everyone else wants you to have this baby. Antenatal classes run by hospitals tend to promote a highly medicalised approach to childbirth, because, after all, that's what they have to offer. At the hospital we went to, hatchet-faced midwives who had trained in women's prisons advertised the joys of the epidural and the simple pleasures of the emergency Cæsarean. Until they had a woman plugged in to half a dozen machines going bleep, they felt their job was only half done. Natural childbirth, they made it clear, was for poofs and wimps who couldn't hack it in the real world. A dozen couples sat in a circle, scarcely daring to breathe, hoping the midwives wouldn't pick on them. This was childbirth as if the Kray twins had been running it. As far as these midwives were concerned, bringing a defenceless baby into the world was just a part of their job. Terrorising parents was the fun bit.

What a contrast to the antenatal classes organised by the National Childbirth Trust. These were in someone's house and involved sundry cups of herbal tea and chocolate biscuits. We had to take off our shoes and sit on bean bags. Where was the giant spliff? Did Jimi Hendrix have a new album out? A mere twelve of us were at this one, which wiped out Tuesday evenings for only eight weeks. This week, dilation of the cervix. Next week, Braxton-Hicks contractions. It was a gruelling course, chocolate HobNobs notwithstanding. But by the end of it we knew more about childbirth than we had thought possible, and far more than many of us had wanted to know. Our host and teacher was a tiny self-effacing woman called Val, who had no particular qualifications as far as we knew, other than having had loads of kids. We could hear them running around in the kitchen and upstairs and in and out of the house (either that or she had a hell of a problem with rats). Val's was the voice of experience. She had been there. She knew what it was like. We respected what she had to say. Also, for the class she had knitted several female body parts, which the men liked to play with. It was the nearest some of us would come to sex for a very long time.

The NCT is a registered charity which was founded in 1957 to help parents and parents-to-be, and now helps around 300,000 of them a year, through antenatal classes, helplines, social events and a suitably well-stocked website. Its information, it says, is based on objective research evidence, and it would disavow any allegations of bias in favour of natural childbirth. Its aim is purely to give people the facts. Even so, you won't usually find NCT antenatal teachers suggesting you have a Cæsarean just for the fun of it. Val was an unabashed fan of natural childbirth.

This is an unusually appealing ideology, or religion, or whatever you want to call it. As parents-to-be, we had passed the first months of the pregnancy in a haze of suppressed terror. Now, we were ripe for ideological reprogramming. All we craved was a little certainty. A skilful antenatal class teacher could supply this, as well as gallons of nettle tea. Val was just what we needed. Her unusually hairy armpits positively reeked of common sense.

The theory and practice of natural childbirth are based around the belief that, for most women, childbirth is a safe and simple process that doctors and their machines have over-complicated. It was pioneered in the 1970s by the French obstetrician Michel Odent, when what he called 'industrialised obstetrics' had become the norm. Forget forceps and drugs, said Odent. Forget bleeping machines in cruelly overlit, soulless delivery rooms. At his own birth centre outside Paris, Odent would encourage mothers to give birth in darkened rooms, maybe with a few candles burning, with tapes of their favourite music playing, possibly even whalesong if the local record shops hadn't run out. In hospitals they would lie a woman on a bed as though there was someone wrong with her. In a natural childbirth, she would be more likely to give birth squatting or kneeling or hanging by her fingertips from the lampshade, if that's what made her comfortable. Odent pioneered water births, of which more later. And he avoided medical intervention unless it was absolutely necessary. His ideas were simple, obvious and profoundly controversial.

For a lot of obstetricians have no time for this at all. They believe that childbirth has been civilised by technological advance. No longer do women die in childbirth – or at least, very rarely (in England and Wales in 1907, 3,520 women died in childbirth, or as a direct consequence of being pregnant. In 1997 the figure was 38. That's 0.059 for every 1,000 births. They are more likely to be killed in a road accident on the way to the hospital). Drugs take away the pain. And if they want, women can subcontract the whole process to the surgeons by having an elective Cæsarean. An increasing number of middle-class women, it says in the newspapers, are 'too posh to push'. Maybe they have to be back at their desks in two weeks and so don't have time for all this pregnancy stuff. Or maybe it all seems too much like hard work. Far easier to have the little blighter sliced out and turned over straightaway to the first of eleven Bosnian *au pairs* who will be caring for it 23 hours and 40 minutes a day until it's packed off to school in seven years. According to one eminent obstetrician, these women 'know the risks. But the way I see it, they are like people who choose to travel by car rather than train – despite knowing the train is safer.' In the US, Cæsareans are actually promoted as a lifestyle choice. One hospital ad encourages mothers-to-be to 'keep yourself honeymoon fresh with a Cæsarean'. As it happens, women having Cæsareans are four times more likely to suffer serious complications than women giving birth vaginally, and nearly twice as likely to have problems conceiving again. No one really knows the long-term risks involved in delivery by forceps (every bit as nasty as it sounds) or ventouse (the giant sink plunger of your worst nightmares). But according to Department of Health figures, more than half of all births in NHS hospitals now involve forceps, ventouse or Cæsarean section.

Not that natural childbirth rejects medical intervention altogether – of course not. If an emergency Cæsarean is needed, an emergency Cæsarean it will be. One of the man-eating midwives at the hospital's antenatal class sneeringly called this 'the best of both worlds', which is true – and a strong endorsement for natural childbirth, I would have thought. Why not have the best of both worlds, if it's available and free?

These, then, are the opposing ideologies. Their battleground is the antenatal class. Woollen wombs and flip charts are the main weaponry, and the poor embattled parents-to-be are the first wave of troops to be mown down in the crossfire. You have to wonder what sort of people would willingly let themselves in for this misery. Then you look in the mirror. In some NCT classes, I have heard, everyone becomes terribly good friends, and are at each other's births and invite each other to dinner parties and become godparents to each other's children and play sad wife-swapping games and divorce horribly and drink themselves to death in sorry bedsits in wind-battered seaside towns. And it's true, there is a camaraderie of sorts. You are all there together, a slight nervousness unsuccessfully masking your deep-seated fear, and exactly half of you have had to cancel something more interesting to come to this. You couldn't fail to get on. Whether these bonds last beyond the end of the classes is less certain. Like holiday friendships, they may or may not survive the flight home.

For now, however, you are stuck in a room with these people, learning about labour. (Once you have learned it you will know it forever, setting you apart in yet another way from your baby-free friends.) The mothers-to-be you will already have sized up. Opinions differ over precisely when pregnant women are at their foxiest, but let's assume that two of them are highly fanciable and another three aren't bad at all. (The names of the others you will fail to remember throughout the eight weeks of the course.) Sadly, none of them will notice you. They are already pregnant and their need for a man has lapsed. Also, their actual man is sitting next to them. To look round for a replacement before the baby was born would be indiscreet. Let them see that

Junior has inherited Dad's huge flappy ears and weak chin before they start wondering who it'll be next time. (You can see that it's but a short route to that sorry bedsit in the wind-battered seaside town.)

So let us leave the mothers-to-be for now. Let us turn our attention instead to the men. At your first antenatal class everybody will introduce themselves – with forenames only, as though they were at an AA meeting. 'I am Marcus ...' [huge pause to pluck up courage] '... and I am going to be a father.' In fact, you might as well be at an AA meeting for all the chance you have of getting a drink. (Similarly, at the end of the session, absolutely nobody will say, 'So who fancies a quick half at the pub on the corner?' Eyebrows would be raised, tuts would be tutted. This is female territory, and you have to be on your best behaviour.)

Take a quick look around the room. Not all men are easy to categorise, but this lot will be.

- Mr Enthusiastic. He is listening to every word and taking lots of notes. He and his wife Jane (or possibly Rebecca) stare lovingly into each other's eyes every eight minutes to show everyone how much they are still in love. On Thursday afternoons he and a girl from Marketing have angry sex in a nearby Holiday Inn.

- Mr Busy. He makes it clear that he has just come from an important meeting, and hints that he has another one immediately afterwards. This is just habit, as he and his wife are actually intending to go home and ring for a curry. He comes straight from work, burping surreptitiously from time to time, and occasionally asks aggressive and wrong-headed questions of the antenatal class teacher, just to prove to the other men that he is too important to pay attention properly. He refuses to switch off his mobile phone, and then when he takes a call, pretends it's from New York. He will be sick with fear during the birth, and then rush off at the earliest opportunity to an important meeting.

- Mr Youthful. He and his wife Mrs Youthful are the youngest people in the room and very conscious of the fact. Mrs Youthful listens carefully and tries not to cry. Mr Youthful, who is also trying not to cry, looks at his feet and says very little. He will eat two thirds of the chocolate HobNobs.

- Mr Old. He has been through all this before. She may be his second wife, or even his third. He is happy to share the benefit of his considerable experience with anyone who asks. No one asks, so he shares it anyway. His new wife looks on admiringly. The antenatal class teacher waits patiently for him to stop talking. Then less patiently. The one thing Mr Old doesn't say is that he hasn't been allowed to see his first two children, by law, since 1986.

- Mr Cool. Unlike most of the other men there, Mr Cool has worked out how to play this thing, but then he is Mr Cool. Listening carefully, nodding sagely, occasionally offering intelligent comments, Mr Cool appears to have embraced his fate head on. But what he is really thinking is that he is better dressed than all these other men, and very much cooler. Whether or not he and his partner go home and shout and argue into the small hours like everyone else, you'll never find out.

- Mr Not There At All. He turns up once, at around week three, then disappears permanently. All the other men hate his guts. The mother of his child tells the group that he has gone on an extended and important business trip. In fact he is at home with his wife.

Most of the men who do turn up will have one and only one thought bouncing around inside their skulls: Do I Really Need To Be Here? It's an impossible question to answer. Your conscience may have something to say about it. The mother of your child may have, too. But if you are at all curious about what's going on, antenatal classes can be very useful. The first big surprise is the sheer quantity of stuff there is to learn. You quickly realise that not only do you know almost nothing about any of this, but that whatever you find out now, it probably won't be enough. It's like those dreams we all have of sitting in an exam for something important and having nothing to write on the paper because, for one reason or another, you haven't quite got round to doing any academic work in living memory. The fear of being found out afflicts most adults, especially those who haven't been found out yet. Parents, schools, universities, employers and girlfriends never managed it; maybe childbirth is your Waterloo.

As the husband, partner or convenient male appendage of

the mother-to-be, your role in the birth will be far more prominent than you might have expected, or wished. Like most fathers-to-be, I had been hoping that, when it all happened, I would be able to stand on the sidelines and offer everyone well-meaning advice without actually doing anything very much. Antenatal classes put me right. When labour begins your beloved will turn into a screaming, sweating, pain-crazed creature from the Black Lagoon, and all responsibility will devolve to you. Even Mr Cool gulped when he heard this.

For there are many decisions to be made, before, during and even after the birth (such as what to do with the afterbirth). Do you want the birth at home or in hospital? In water or on dry land? Do you want all the drugs medicine has to offer, or will you try for a natural birth? Do you want a birth partner present? How do you feel about Cæsareans? In each of these questions I use 'you' to mean 'you and your partner', which effectively means 'your partner', as it's unlikely you feel strongly about any of these things. How can you? It's not your body. (If you are deeply paranoid it's not your baby either until the DNA test comes through.) Quite reasonably, it is your partner who will end up making most of these decisions. Your job as she makes them is to nod your head and look thoughtful. Later on you will have to remember what these decisions were – a challenge in itself – and then act on them. Remember that you are only the junior executive in this management structure. Kaz Cooke, in her *Rough Guide To Pregnancy And Birth*, tells of a man asking an antenatal class teacher exactly what his role should be during labour. Her reply: 'Do whatever she tells you and be quick about it.'

● Home or hospital. Home has many advantages. It has a kettle, and a fridge. It has your bed, on which you can lie down for a nap while she is downstairs heaving and grunting with the midwife and there's nothing much for you to do. You can smoke at home, if you smoke. You can start smoking, if you don't.

Unfortunately, the NHS doesn't have much time for home births. GPs discourage them (more work for them), and some midwives are less than enthusiastic (more work for them). As birth has become more medicalised, home births have become rarer. In 1965, 28.6 per cent of births in the UK were at home. 20 years later it was down to 0.9 per cent. These days the rate has risen to about two per cent, thanks to natural childbirthers, but it's still considered unusual to the point of eccentricity.

Most first-time parents, though, opt for hospital births: it just seems safer, somehow. Even after 73 antenatal classes you will only have the sketchiest idea of what is going to happen. You will need to be reassured through this deeply mysterious and mildly terrifying experience, and for most of us that means the bleeping machines, obstetricians in white coats, midwives on tap and unlimited supplies of that five-ply green paper they always mop things up with. If you are thinking of having another baby one day (you aren't, but she will be) you can have a home birth then. Second time around you will have some idea of what to expect, and if you were planning to get the place redecorated anyway, so much the better.

● Water or dry land? Now here's a tricky one. All common sense suggests that a water birth would be messy, dangerous and stressful, and the preference of hippies and show-offs. None of this is true, other than the hippies and show-offs bit. In fact, babies seem to love being born in water. They are in no danger, as their little lungs don't start working until they get their little tap on the arse from the midwife. And warm water is wonderful pain relief for the mother. Floating about like a whale will help reduce the pressure on her abdomen, and she can move more easily into different positions. Also, if you have your trunks handy, you too can have a dip, as long as you don't do anything silly like dive in or do a sneaky pee in the water.

The main disadvantage is administrative. Water births can be hard work to fix up, which means hard work for you. More and more hospitals are installing facilities for water births – big deep circular baths of a type often advertised during Countdown for the elderly and infirm. They are excellent, and therefore much in demand. In theory you should be able to book them in advance. In practice, when you arrive in the hospital at four in the morning, you get what's offered, and someone else has always blagged the water birth room first. You can always elect to have a water birth at home, which, I can say from experience, is fantastic – but again, might be more trouble than it's worth for first-birthers. For it is none other than you, the father-to-be, who will have to build and fill the fucker, almost certainly in the middle of the night. Something to keep your mind occupied, maybe. A little too much to keep your mind occupied, I found. The instructions said it would take 15 to 20 minutes to build. It took me an hour and a half.

Dry land is the default option. Popular amongst frequent

flyers and survivors of major maritime disasters, it's what nearly everybody does. And yet when someone has a baby in a film, they still call for towels. So what's the difference?[6]

● Drugs or natural childbirth? Another awkward one, although this really is the mother's decision. Some women stagger into hospital screaming for epidurals. Others have spent so long practising their yoga that they can keep the pain at bay throughout labour. Everyone is different. No one is better than anyone else. And whatever she decides, you can't even begin to contribute. You're not actually in pain, unless she has inadvertently punched you on the way to the hospital. Or intentionally. It's possible. Remember, it's all your fault.

In fact, all you need to do here is follow instructions. Do what she says, and be prepared for her to change her mind at the last minute, as may well happen. You have to be light on your feet to get through this childbirth business.

● Posture. According to one eminent authority it was Louis XIV of France, the Sun King, who first came up with the idea of women giving birth on their backs with their legs up in the air in stirrups. There was no medical reason for it. Louis simply wanted a good view when his children came into the world, and

---

6. Note that some proponents of medicalised childbirth are instinctively hostile to water births; one or two even warn against it. Their main concern is that a baby can gasp as it is born, which could lead to respiratory distress. But this is extremely rare. The mortality rate for water births is actually lower than that for dry-land births. If you and your partner decide that it's for you, do not be deterred by trumped-up 'safety' arguments.

couldn't be bothered to bend down and look between his wife's legs. Somehow, though, the practice caught on, and these days it's doctors and midwives who can't be bothered to bend over. It's easier for everyone in hospital if the patient lies down and behaves, but it may be easier for the mother-to-be if she ignores this convention and squats on the floor as everyone used to. For thousands of years women squatted when giving birth, because it was the natural and obvious thing to do. In ancient Egypt the hieroglyphic for 'birth' shows a woman squatting and a baby's head poking out of her vagina. The ancient Romans invented the birthing stool, with a hole cut away for the baby to fall through. Squatting uses that most valuable of natural forces, gravity. If your partner wishes to squat rather than lie down, she must be allowed to. And if she changes her mind five minutes later and wants to lie down, she must be allowed to do that as well.

● Birth partner. This is a terrific idea, borrowed from primitive societies, or somewhere else, I forget which. When your beloved gives birth, you will be there, and a midwife will be there and, if you both so decide, a previously appointed birth partner will be there as well, to lend a hand and give support and hold hands and give her massage and do all the things you thought you'd be doing.

Yes, seriously.

The thinking is rigorously practical. Neither you nor the mother-to-be are likely to have been through this before, and the midwife, for all her experience and sympathy, could be a complete stranger. So by bringing along someone else who knows the ropes, the mother-to-be will feel more secure and the father-to-be won't feel overwhelmed by the burden of responsibility for absolutely everything, which is the way it feels at the moment. She (the birth partner isn't usually a man, and if it is, you may start to wonder why) will probably have kids of her own. She shouldn't be the mother-to-be's own mother, as that relationship will be more loaded with baggage than carousel 'A' in Heathrow Terminal Two. She should be a mate, someone your beloved can trust, someone who – let's be brutal here – isn't you. Unless you're an Alpha Male and like to be in charge all the time, these words should give you a Ready Brek glow of contentment. Someone to share the shit – as one father told me, 'it's the best idea to hit childbirth since afterbirth paté'. Better, some of us might say.

● Music at the birth? Candles? Whalesong? One of the main tenets of natural childbirth is that the atmosphere must be right – which is to say calm and relaxed rather than panicked and terror-stricken. So, if you are taking a portable CD player, try and take quiet, restful music rather than, shall we say, AC/DC's *Back In Black*. Fathers in neighbouring birthing rooms have been known to turn up the volume to drown out each other's music, behaviour that may speed up the birth but will also later be cited in divorce proceedings. Let her choose the music. If you really don't like Nanci Griffith, that's tough.

Candles are good fun, as they need lighting again after you've blown them all out with one mighty puff. Avoid scented candles – more than half a dozen of these in the same room are deemed to be an instrument of torture by the Geneva Convention.

But essential oils can be amazingly helpful, and calm things right down. (Homoeopathic remedies are also worth looking into: they can be of use before, during and especially after the birth.)

Whalesong is available on CD and cassette from all good whalesong stockists. Particularly useful if she's expecting to give birth to a whale.

Having made these decisions, you and your beloved will make a Birth Plan. This is a document that outlines your requirements and preferences for the birth. If you're lucky the midwife will read it before putting it in a file. If you're really unlucky she will set fire to it in front of your face.

8

what you need to know, what you need to do

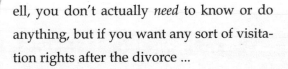

Well, you don't actually *need* to know or do anything, but if you want any sort of visitation rights after the divorce ...

PREMATURE BIRTH

Don't worry too much about this. Ninety-three per cent of pregnancies go to full term or beyond. Indeed, a first baby is more likely to stay in there too long than pop out too early. It's warm in the womb, and the food is good. You would stay in there if you could. Babies are not stupid, as you will soon discover.

BRAXTON-HICKS CONTRACTIONS

For some reason, this is just about the only thing that all men remember from their antenatal classes, possibly because it sounds like a firm of builders. Braxton-Hicks are the Phoney War of contractions. They can start at about six months, may occur more frequently in the final weeks, and mean precisely nothing. Oddly enough, sex can bring them on. Semen contains prostaglandin hormones, rather larger quantities of which are often given to women when they are overdue. Which is why midwives also recommend sex to hurry things along a bit. This is the only other thing all men remember from their antenatal classes: it's the excuse many have been waiting for for several months.

YOGA, BREATHING EXERCISES, MEDITATION

She may go to special classes for these, and you will probably have to practise them with her at antenatal classes as well. Unless you're the sort of hyper-committed dad you read about in annoying books, this will probably be a bit of a chore. At worst it will be an embarrassing and annoying chore that will cause you to shout at each other like Italians. Try and remain calm: this is just part of your punishment. If you do drop off during any of the exercises, try not to snore: it goes down very badly.

BIRTH POSITIONS

In TV soaps women lie on beds and open their legs. In real life, many women will prefer other more comfortable positions: squatting, kneeling, hanging from ropes, doing a handstand while humming songs from the shows. Some of these require you to be right behind her holding her up or supporting her in some way. *This may be the worst thing of all about birth.* The phrase 'heavily pregnant', you'll have noticed, starts with 'heavily'. Even Kate Moss weighed a ton in the ninth month. No one will care how much it hurts you. Your back muscles are expendable. Letters from your doctor or your mother excusing you from games will be ignored. In the weeks leading up to the birth, you will have to practise these agonising positions until you drop. Sportsmen, who know exactly how to feign injuries, should be prepared to twinge that hamstring or strain that groin with about three weeks to go. Non-sportsmen should start on the weights, or prepare to hire lifting equipment. (Water births spare you all this – another significant advantage.)

IRRITABILITY

It's in all the books. Women get irritable in the last stages of pregnancy. Having read this, irritatingly, it gives them permission to be irritable. Chicken or egg? Stay in the pub an hour or two longer and you'll find out.

NESTING INSTINCT

Another sign that the baby is on its way. She will be full of energy and may start frantically cleaning the house. This is pure instinct. She wants to get things ready for the baby. Suggest she relays the floor and paints the window frames while she is about it.

CURRY

As well as sex, an excellent way for her to hurry things along a bit is a blisteringly hot curry. Whole belief systems could be built around this delightful fact. Managers of Indian restaurants, however, may be less than keen to see yet another hugely pregnant woman waddling in. Their hot towels are for mopping your face after the meal, nothing more. Order a takeaway instead.

MORE OLD WIVES' TALES

Other sure-fire ways to induce labour: drink castor oil, get an enema, stimulate the nipples. Or if she is an Olympic gymnast, all three at the same time.

Bear in mind, though, that old wives also hold that if a pregnant woman wears high-heels, the baby will be cross-eyed; that a hare-lip is caused by the foetus sucking its thumb in the womb; and that if a child is born with teeth, it's a sign of syphilis. As it happens, Napoleon Bonaparte and Julius Caesar were born with teeth. So was Richard III.

And yet there is one old wives' tale that large numbers of

apparently functional people still believe to be true. Ancient relatives will have it on excellent authority that a pregnant woman should never raise her arms above her head, as it increases the probability of miscarriage, and can cause the foetus to be strangled by its umbilical cord. Absolute poppycock. If she raises her arms above her head, people will be able to tickle her armpits. Can she take that risk? Only she can decide.

COUVADE

This is the phenomenon, observed in many primitive tribes, of fathers undergoing a sort of sympathetic pregnancy, sharing labour pains, taking to their beds for days on end and sometimes even acting out childbirth. Couvade means 'hatching' in French, although that's the last thing likely to happen. It was first noticed in Corsica in the first century AD, and the Witoto tribe of the Amazon are among several who keep the flames of couvade alive. It wouldn't happen here ... would it? As it happens, studies suggest that between a fifth and a quarter of all fathers-to-be experience pregnancy-related symptoms: toothache, gastrointestinal symptoms and even weight gain. Can we blame getting hugely fat on our partner's having a baby? We certainly can.

PACKING THE BAG

Make sure you've got the following inside:

- All the hospital notes, including copy of birth plan if not already burnt by midwife.

- Loads of clothes for her. Big T-shirt or nightdress, pair of socks, pair of slippers, dressing gown, big pants (yummy!), enormous nursing bras (yowsah!) and thong (joke). Also: more toiletries than she'll ever need, bath towels, hot water bottle, bottle of mineral water and hand mirror so she can see baby's head popping out if she really wants to. Plus: super-strength sanitary pads (extra-large), kitchen sink, sponges, face flannels, box of disposable breast pads, water spray bottle to cool her skin, portable CD player, *The Best Of Nanci Griffith*, copy of *Hello!* magazine plus all that stuff that lives at the bottom of handbags, undisturbed by human hand from one generation to the next. Better let her pack all this up for herself.

- For baby, you'll need a vest or two, a couple of romper suits, some nappies (size 1), nappy changing equipment, hat, socks and a blanket or shawl to wrap the little shivering creature in.

- For you, take a change of clothes, as labour wards can be fearsomely hot (and the clothes you're wearing may get covered in something nasty); sandwiches, fruit, biscuits, water, hip flask, cool box with beer in; camera, camcorder, extra film, extra battery; phone card, address book containing important phone numbers, pile of pound coins (you can't use mobile phones in hospitals); good book; pillow; noose.

They say you should pack the bag at about 36 weeks, but you'll probably pack it at the last minute like everybody else.

LABOUR

How will you know that labour has started? Because it's the worst possible moment for it. Either she's in Safeway's, or you're drunk, or both. More often than not, it's in the middle of the night.

- The 'show'. There's a little mucus plug that seals the cervix during pregnancy. When it pops out, she'll have a pinkish-brown discharge about the size of a 20p piece which, by ancient showbiz tradition, is called the 'show'. Something is stirring, but there's no need to do anything yet (other than panic).

- The waters break. In TV dramas this always happens in the back of a cab or some other humorous location. It isn't definitive evidence that labour is starting, although it won't be far away. What has happened is that the amniotic sac has ruptured. Fluid can trickle, or as in disaster films it can surge. Call the midwife or delivery room for advice, but they will probably tell you to stay put until labour really gets going.

- Contractions. Imagine a dull, clutching ache in your stomach that lasts a few seconds and goes away. Then imagine another one in 15 or 20 minutes' time. What's the big deal? But once this process has begun, there's not much that can stop it. Baby is raring to go, the womb tightens, and with each throb the cervix dilates a little bit further. Soon the pain phases will get longer and the gaps between them shorter. And still there's no need to go to hospital. They say that if she can talk lucidly on the phone to the hospital, it's probably too early to go in. Only when the contractions last about a minute, and are coming every five to ten minutes, should you hotfoot it for the delivery room. The midwife will check that the mother-to-be is three centimetres dilated, and if she is, that's when labour officially starts. Synchronise your watches. All timings start here.

EXAMINATIONS

Medicine, as we all know, is hugely advanced and highly technological. So what's the best way of checking how far the cervix has dilated? It's the same for midwives and doctors and everyone: put on a rubber glove, stick your hand up, have a good poke around. It's as though a peaceful country lane has been upgraded to a four-lane bypass. If they've put a Little Chef halfway up, don't be at all surprised.

THE THREE STAGES OF LABOUR

Stage one is when the contractions pull the cervix open. Stage two is when the baby is born. Stage three is when the afterbirth comes out. It might all take a couple of hours. It might take several days.

- Stage One. This can last up to twelve hours, or even longer with a first baby. As baby's skull thumps against cervix, in its first recorded act of headbanging, your beloved may start thinking about pain relief, in between screaming. All fathers think: God, I'm so glad I'm not going through this.

● Stage Two. Once the cervix is fully dilated (ten centimetres) the baby says a tearful goodbye to the womb and is pushed through the birth canal. 'Push! Push!' says the midwife. Think of Thunderbird 1 rolling down on its little runway to the lift-off point. Then Scott Tracy fires up the engines and out surges Baby into the world. This stage can take two hours or a few minutes. All fathers think: this is the bit they always show on TV.

● Stage Three. Of interest primarily to gourmets and Dr Hannibal Lecter, the placenta, or afterbirth, will emerge half an hour or so later. Compared to the previous stages this one is almost painless. The real surprise is how big the placenta is. It's as though your partner has had a joint of beef up there for the past few months. All fathers think: I don't care what anyone says, I'm not eating that.

PAIN RELIEF

Few of the usual drugs you'd get in hospital, or even at the chemist, can be used, as they may affect the baby. More subtle approaches are required. In ascending order of usefulness, they are:

● The TENS machine. Electrodes are taped to her back and give her short sharp shocks of current which stimulate the production of endorphins, the body's natural painkillers. Apparently it's rather pleasant. You can also hire one of these to use at home in the early stages of labour. TENS stands for Transcutaneous

Electrical Nerve Stimulation, a fact to kill any conversation stone dead.

● Gas and Air. Also trades under the name Entonox. It's a mixture of oxygen and nitrous oxide, and she will breathe it in through a mask. This one is all about timing: she must start using it as soon as she feels a contraction starting, as it takes about 20 seconds to kick in. If you ever see a father-to-be in a labour ward banging his head against a wall, he is either in the last stages of terminal despair, or took a mouthful of gas and air 30 seconds ago and wants to see if it'll work.

● Pethidine. Rather strong morphine-based drug not much liked by natural childbirthers, as it can pass through the placental wall and make the baby drowsy. Pethidine doesn't dull the pain so much as fuck with your head in true opiate style so that you're not aware of the pain, or anything else for that matter. Will it make your child a heroin addict in later life? Find out in a couple of decades' time.

● Epidural. This is the famed Full Monty of medicalised birth procedure. The anaesthetist sticks a needle into the spinal column, and anaesthetises womb, vagina, vulva, everything. They'll usually keep a drip going so that the anaesthetic can be topped up. Advantages: no pain at all, can read *Hello!* magazine sitting up in bed as baby is born. Risks: the mother may injure herself during stage two simply because she feels no pain and so doesn't know what's going on down there. Also, if it doesn't quite work, there's the tiniest, faintest possibility that she will be numbed on one side of her body, and feel everything on the other side, which, I hear, is freakishly unpleasant. Unbelievably small risk: permanent paralysis if anaesthetist cocks it up. It's very rare, and no one I have met has ever heard of anyone this has happened to (one writer has said that it's about as likely as being hit by a jumbo jet). And yet it's such a horrific prospect it puts many mothers off epidurals altogether. (When you mention this to certain doctors, steam often billows from their ears. They think epidurals are just fantastic, but it's not they who have to have the enormous needle stuck into the small of their back, is it?)

VIDEO CAMERA

Very useful, and you won't regret bringing it, but on no account should you (a) say things like 'Action!' (b) ask the midwife to move aside so you can get a better view, or (c) suggest a retake. Also, watch out for stray splashes – they can clog up the mechanism forever.

WIRING UP THE DELIVERY ROOM SO THAT THE WHOLE BIRTH CAN BE SEEN LIVE ON THE INTERNET

Get out. Get out of this book right now.

TURD

It happens. She won't be able to help it. She is using many of the same muscles: expelling a baby, expelling a giant turd, comes to the same thing. Midwives, fortunately, are used to it. But you may never forget it. For one thing it's a noise like none other – or more precisely, a combination of noises. The rumble of herding bison? The rumble of herding bison with incontinence problems caught in a sudden thunderstorm? Wire the room for sound, and you'll be able to work it out later when you have time to think about it properly.

SWEARING

At some point they always start shouting and swearing at you because it's all your fault. Finally their true feelings emerge. Convention demands that you take it on the chin and say nothing. Revenge is a dish best eaten cold – not unlike afterbirth paté.

For this is her last fling. When the baby is born she must become the perfect mother, coo sweetly to her newborn and sacrifice everything to its health and well-being. Now is her last chance to be the centre of attention and assault you with her fists. And the fact that you are expecting it gives her licence to behave even more badly. For fathers, it's the reverse. You are doing your gentle and self-sacrificing bit now, when it's needed. You can go back to being a self-centred bastard when it's all over. So let her have her moment.

FOOD AND DRINK

All this hanging around can make a man hungry. Unfortunately, labour etiquette demands that you be on hand at all times. Your partner needs to believe that you are directing every particle of your attention at her, despite the deafening rumble emanating from your stomach. Should you have eaten before you came? It doesn't matter if you did, because most labours go on so long you could fit in three square meals and still have room for a bag of crisps. Most men feign impossibly weak bladders, sneak out of the door and then go in search of a vending machine. This will be nearly empty, with only the nastiest crisp flavours left and a very elderly Bounty bar that appears to be moving. You mull over the choice. It's lovely just to be out of the room. Some fathers-to-be can stand in front of a hospital vending machine for up to 20 minutes. It could be the last peace you ever know.

WHO'S WHO AT A HOSPITAL BIRTH

For most of the time it'll just be you and her and the midwife and the birth partner if you have one. For long periods even the midwife won't be there. She will be next door reading the paper. (Fair enough: there's nothing else for her to do.) Then, unless it's a very quick labour, your midwife's shift will come to an end. She will look at her watch, sidle out of the room with a little wave and sprint down the corridor cheering madly. And a new midwife will come in, a stranger, and all that effort you put into bonding with the old midwife, all that flattery and small talk and the flowers and the chocolates – it will all have been wasted.

You will have to start again from scratch. This can be one of the most dispiriting moments in the whole ghastly business.

Then stage two begins and after hours of relative solitude, the delivery room will suddenly be more crowded than Charing Cross station. Who are all these people? There may be an obstetrician, an anaesthetist, another midwife or two, possibly a nurse, the cleaner (who has come to watch), some students, a TV production team making a fly-on-the-wall documentary, lawyers, management, a worried-looking family of four who got out of the lift at the wrong floor and have come to ask directions. Perhaps you should have sold tickets.

HELL ON EARTH

Everyone tells you how wonderful this all is. What a magical experience it is. How you'll never forget it as long as you live. Well, one out of three isn't bad.

The grim, brutal truth is that childbirth is that cruellest of combinations: it is stressful and it is boring. Childbirth is hours and hours of unceasing teeth-grinding anxiety. It is also so tedious you will want to cry. The good bit is at the end. Partly this is because you have a gorgeous little baby who may look a bit like you. But mainly it's because it's all over.

This is the great unspoken truth of childbirth. No one is allowed to mention it. Other fathers don't say anything. You won't either. It's against the rules. And one of the reasons no one mentions it is that mothers aren't supposed to know. They will know, immediately after the birth and possibly for a few months afterwards. But later they will forget. They are biologically compelled to wipe it from their memories, for if they could recall it, they would never do it again. Do not blame them for it is not their fault. It's your fault, as I keep telling you.

'I CAN'T COPE'

She will say these words at some point as well. There will be terror in her eyes. For all her preparation, there will have been no readying her for what labour is actually like. And she knows, and you know, that she can't wriggle out of it now. All you can do is reassure her, and love her, and tell her she's wonderful and brave and strong, and she can do it. Ideally, fathers should be able to practise this flannel during antenatal classes. Nonetheless, whether you realise it or not, a lifetime of watching Clint Eastwood films has prepared you for this moment. Narrow your eyes. Let your jaw become granite. Chew on a match if you have one handy. Say what needs to be said and show not a scintilla of weakness. It's your strength she needs. Go on punk, make my day.

IT'S NOT LIKE IT IS ON TV

It really isn't. In some genuinely useful and interesting research, Sarah Clement of Guy's and St Thomas's Hospital in London analysed 92 births seen in one year of TV drama. Of these, four babies and one mother died in childbirth, while another five babies and four mothers experienced life-threatening complications. All these figures are way, way beyond statistical likelihood.

In around a third of the TV births labour was so unexpected that either it happened in a strange place or people who should have been there weren't, and the whole thing was over in a trice. And in virtually all the births there was no pain relief: gas and air, pethidine and epidurals cropped up in seven per cent, three per cent and five per cent of the births respectively. Although my own researches have been less thorough, I should add that I have *never* seen anyone give birth on TV anywhere but on their back; and the mother-to-be just screams a lot, rather than yelling 'You fucking, fucking, fucking fuck!' specifically at the father of her child. And the baby just born is always three months old.

PERSONALITY CLASHES

Midwives are people like anyone else. Some you will love almost carnally. Others you may take a dislike to. The midwife at our first birth was young, stroppy and as nurturing as a velociraptor. She regarded our birth plan with contempt and us with barely disguised hostility. My girlfriend, who had been practising yoga and breathing for weeks, was trying to go through labour without heavy duty pain relief, which is to say TENS machine – yes; gas and air – yes; pethidine – let's hope not; and epidural – not on your nelly. The midwife is supposed to support you, that is her job. This one just said, 'You think you're doing all right now, but you'll be screaming for pain relief before it's all over. Trust me, I only tell the truth.' We were first timers, we were scared stupid, and this vicious little cow made a difficult situation a hundred times worse. Eventually her shift ended and she was replaced by a human being. But by then my girlfriend's confidence had been obliterated and she had had to have pethidine, to which she had a very unpleasant reaction. It's four years on, but if I saw this midwife in the street I still might have to be physically restrained.

Midwives are central to the birth process, and their importance cannot be overstated. The two we had for the second birth were two of the most impressive people I have ever met: fantastically nurturing, very calm, boundlessly experienced and still possessed of a sense of wonder that made every birth interesting and exciting for them. A woman in labour needs emotional support from someone who knows the ropes, and there is no one better placed to do this than a midwife. (There is a chronic shortage of midwives, incidentally. It's not a glamorous area of medicine, possibly because, on the whole, only women do it. But it's one of the most demanding. It demands empathy and wisdom as well as technical skills.)

The point is that if you get a midwife you can't bear - or more pertinently, who can't bear you - you are *entirely within your rights to get her replaced*. Even the first time round, we knew this, and yet our birth partner Jane and I did nothing. Instead, we were cowed into submission. Hospitals do this to you. They institutionalise you, even if you have only been there five minutes. The real surprise was that no amount of preparation - books read, antenatal classes attended - could prepare us for what happened. One malevolent midwife altered the whole experience for everybody - not least for the baby, who was relying on her most of all.

A FEW TECHNICAL TERMS

Pay attention at the back.

- Induction. At 42 or 43 weeks, the baby is technically overdue and you will be encouraged to have it induced. This may involve an artificial hormone called syntocinon, which is powerful stuff. Normal contractions build up gradually, so pain relief can be managed gradually. Syntocinon contractions are immediately intense and painful: 0 to 60 mph in minutes, rather than hours. Induction is not an easy option, and shouldn't be considered lightly. Unless there are strong medical reasons in favour, it may be preferable to wait until the baby is ready to come out of its own accord.

- Breech birth. Baby should be coming out head first. If it's the wrong way round, and it's leading with its buttocks, that's called a breech birth. They may be able to do it vaginally – it may depend on nothing more than the skill and experience of your midwife – but a Cæsarean is more likely. If it is spotted early enough in the scanning process, a breech baby can often be coerced to turn round. (Which only goes to prove that there really is someone alive in there.)

- Forceps. Some births need what will euphemistically be described as 'intervention'. If the baby gets stuck on the way out – its head may be too big, or the cervix may refuse to dilate fully – the famed forceps may be brought into action. The two blades cradle the baby's head, and then someone pulls like billy-o. Warning: forceps are large and scary, and you will never make jokes about them again. Try and ensure that your beloved does not catch sight of them. Why should both of you have night-mares about them for years to come?

● Ventouse. This is a slightly more civilised alternative to the forceps, dating from the 1950s rather than the Spanish Inquisition. It's essentially a sink plunger, inserted carefully up the four-lane bypass and plopped onto the baby's head. Then someone pulls like the devil. Mainly worrying because at this stage in its short life, the baby's skull is very malleable, and at best the ventouse will leave a large bruise. At worst you may feel obliged to call your first-born 'Conehead'. This effect subsides quickly, but never quickly enough. Also: it is not unusual for the vacuum seal between the ventouse and the baby's head to be broken, and this makes another extraordinary noise, like a rhino farting. It sounds as though something horrible has happened, but it hasn't. All they do is put the ventouse back on and give it another go.

● Crowning. When the baby appears at the vaginal opening, it is called crowning. Watch this bit if you can: it is extraordinary.

● Episiotomy. I have to admit that merely typing that word launches a full-blooded shiver down my spine. In theory the vagina should be big and stretchy enough for the baby to come out. That's what it is designed for. But if forceps or ventouse are used, or it's a breech birth, or the baby is a whopper, your beloved may need an episiotomy – a slice through the skin of the perineal floor with a small knife. It will bleed like nothing on earth, and it will hurt as much as it bleeds. Many women say 'No Episiotomy' in their birth plan, but you're relying on the expertise of the midwives and/or doctors, and indeed their personal prejudices. So there may be no real choice. (Although they are supposed to ask the mother's permission before they do it.) 'Natural' tears, i.e. not knife-assisted, tend to heal better. The angle of the cut also makes a difference ... but you don't need to know all this, and you certainly don't need to see it, if you are even a third as squeamish as I am.

THE BIRTH

My own first thoughts were 'Fuck! It's a baby!' God knows what I had thought had been in there all this time. Then, because my girlfriend had had pethidine, it turned out that the baby wasn't breathing.

The next six seconds were the worst of my life.

My girlfriend knew nothing about it, which was just as well.

But I could see the baby being taken to the resuscitation machine in the corner and brought back to life: efficiently, without panic, skilfully. I just stood there and watched it, unable to react or, indeed, breathe.

Four ... five ... six seconds, and then the baby inhaled a gobful of glorious hospital air. And so did I.

CUTTING THE CORD

They will ask you if you want to do this: it's traditional. Many men are delighted to do so. I didn't want to; I can't really tell you why. Possibly, I realised that I had had so little to do with the birth that it seemed little more than a token gesture: The One Thing The Dad Does. But then, I had just experienced the worst six seconds of my life. It was all a bit much. So I said no.

But it's more than symbolic. For nine months the umbilical cord has fed and nurtured the growing foetus. (It is tougher and more gristly than you might expect.) Its length can vary prodigiously – from seven inches to 48 inches. No one knows why. (The average is about 20 inches.) In some tribal societies the cord was believed to have magical properties. It was often ceremonially eaten, or carried as a lucky charm, or buried, or placed in a tree. In some cultures it was carefully preserved and then ritually entombed with its owner when he or she died.

We just throw it in the bin. The foetus is now a baby and out here with us. In a few months it will be able to smile, and not long afterwards it will be able to operate the remote control. So cut the cord if you want to: it is a significant moment. And with one bound the baby was free.

BABY

Blimey. Who's this little person, then?

9
amazing stories

'Birth is the most shocking thing that can happen to anybody. I've seen plenty of horror movies, but this about tops it.' FILM DIRECTOR TIM BURTON ABOUT HIS NEWBORN SON

It's different for everyone. The hippopotamus gives birth underwater. The immediate thing a newborn hippo does is float to the surface and take its first breath of air. The giraffe gives birth standing up. Out comes the baby giraffe, and falls six feet to the ground. A meadow vole is ready to reproduce only 25 days after it is born. It has anything up to 17 litters a year, each of up to eight young.

Humans generally have it much easier, although not always. Gorgias of Epirus was born during the funeral of his mother. The pallbearers heard crying in the coffin. They opened it up to find young Gorgias, who had slipped out of the womb and was not just alive but thoroughly cheesed off.

In 1939, Miss Lima Medina, aged five years, eight months, gave birth to a healthy baby in Lima, Peru. In Alexandria,

Virginia, USA in 1969, an unnamed ten-year-old girl gave birth to a healthy baby boy.

Of multiple births, many strange tales are told. A German liner called *Grosser Kurfurst* sailed from Bremen to New York in 1906. On the voyage, three women gave birth. The woman in first class had one baby, the woman in second class had twins, the woman in third class had triplets. Between 1849 and 1957 anyone who gave birth to triplets in England was entitled to a payment from the Crown of £3.

Of carnivores and primates, the hyena is the only animal other than man not to have a penis bone. A gorilla's penis, when erect, is just two inches long. A spider's penis is at the end of one of its legs. A flatworm's penis comes out of its mouth. It has spikes on it.

Koala bears, as we know, eat eucalyptus leaves. Baby koalas are weaned on a eucalyptus leaf soup that comes out of the mother's anus.

When Pablo Picasso was born, the midwife thought he was stillborn. A physician uncle revived him, reputedly by breathing cigar smoke into his lungs. Thomas Hardy was also thought to be stillborn. Then a nurse saw him move.

Ralph and Carolyn Cummins of Clintwood, Virginia, USA, had five children. Catherine was born on 20 February, 1952. Carol was born on 20 February, 1953. Charles came along on 20 February, 1956, Claudia on 20 February, 1961 and Cecilia on 20 February, 1966. (Ralph clearly got a bit sprightly in May.)

This comes from an encyclopædia of folklore published in Chicago in 1903:

'A child born in January will be laborious,

'In February, will love money much but women more.

'The person born in March will be honest and rather handsome.

'The person born in April will be subject to maladies and will travel to his disadvantage.

'A person born in May will be handsome and amiable,

'In June, will be small of stature and very fond of children,

'In July, will be fat and constant,

'In August, ambitious and courageous,

'In September, strong and prudent,

'In October, will be wicked and inconstant and will have a florid complexion,

'In November, will be a gay deceiver,

'In December, will be of passionate disposition and will devote himself to public affairs.'

In the UK, there's always a higher than average number of births in January, February and March, and a lower than average number in October, November and December.

In England and Wales there are between 1,500 and 2,000 births every day.

DUNCAN: J's birth was remarkably straightforward. Dinah was amazingly together, organised, efficient, informed, so she knew and understood what was going on, and because she works in a medical environment she had an insight into that system, and how they work. There are certain options you can have for the birth and she had gone in and found out what they were and worked out what she wanted to do. So a lot of the responsibility in that respect was taken away from me, which was good. On the morning of the birth she started having contractions about four o'clock in the morning. She got up, left me sleeping, started timing them. Then at six o'clock they were getting closer together, so she woke me up and said, I think we need to go to the hospital. The bags were packed, everything was ready, so we got in the car, drove up there, I was trying to crack a few jokes on the way to keep the mood light-hearted. We were in perfectly good spirits. Got to the hospital, they took us through. Dinah's contractions by then were getting closer and closer together, it was starting to happen. And they said, right, let's go through, they put her in the delivery room, and the midwife came in, a young midwife, who Dinah knew from her training. And she was a really nice girl, it was a good atmosphere, very upbeat. J arrived remarkably straightforwardly at ten past twelve – about four hours after we'd got to the hospital. Gas and air was all Dinah had. She'd suffered at the point of delivery, of course, but the whole thing was about as simple as they come, I think. The cord was around J's neck when she came out, but I remember the midwife quickly whipping the cord off, very efficiently, no bother at all. Wrapped her up, brought her over, and I remember us just being really excited and feeling really happy. I must say, I do remember thinking afterwards that I was glad it wasn't any longer than four hours because I was starting to get fed up. I was pleased it was quick, because some people are there for days, aren't they? But it was lovely, really was. The process felt really satisfying. It was quite special. I felt completely happy about it at that point.

GUY: I got a call from Gina saying, 'I think I'm going into labour.' So I went home to pick her up. For the first baby you're fully prepared with a packed bag, complete with two packets of digestives to see me through the night. We drove on to the hospital, and I think I was quite fraught, because when we were only five minutes away, with Gina screaming in agony in the passenger seat, I said to her, 'I think I've left the iron on.' And I insisted on turning round, going back home, which was about five miles, to check that I hadn't left the iron on, while Gina was almost giving birth in the car. And that was my main manifestation of nerves on the day of the birth. I think otherwise I was reasonably calm and collected ...

And then in the actual labour, N got stuck, so she was a Caesarean, and that was pretty scary. You think you've just about plucked up enough courage to stomach watching a natural birth, and then a doctor says, 'Oh, we're going to whip her out by Caesarean, do you want to come and watch?' And you think, mm, I'm not sure I'm really up to seeing my wife being sliced in half, but I suppose I'll have to. So I did. I didn't watch that much, because they erect a sort of sheet, because Gina was conscious during this. She had opted, in typical Gina style, not to have a general anaesthetic, so that she would be awake when the baby came out. So they put a sheet up so she couldn't see herself being cut open. I was with her at the head end, but occasionally looking around the sheet to see what was going on. Basically, push the stomach to one side, push the small intestine to the other side, reach in and ... well, it was a bit like scraping vanilla out of a bucket in an ice cream van. They scraped this child out. The whole thing was pretty ... scary.

So that first one was reasonably traumatic and memorable, and

Gina contrasts it with P's [their third]. I was quite attentive for the first one, mopping Gina's brow, bringing her water and things, being very protective of her, and making sure all the various things on our birth plan were done. When P was born, which was an early evening birth. I went in, and there was a football match I wanted to watch, so I watched football on television for the first hour and a half while she was in labour. I then stole her pillow and blanket and went to sleep in an armchair and had to be woken up by the nurse about five minutes before Gina was due to give birth, because I had slept through five hours of labour, even though Gina was screaming a few feet away.

And O, as the middle child – of course neither of us have any memories whatsoever of how O was born, so she might have been delivered by DHL one day, we really don't remember. She was also the child that we didn't bother to name for three weeks. Because middle children just lose out, I think. Not that we knew at the time she was going to be a middle child.

FERGUS: The first birth reminded me of waiting for a delayed flight. Same sort of plasticky chairs, same feeling of tiredness and lots of magazines to read, and vaguely feeling that you should be doing something to speed things up, but not really knowing what to do. You feel very supernumerary. You feel very much that you are not the focus.

And the second one I was fine with that because we had a doula[7], who was a very good friend of both of ours. She basically

7. A sort of professional birth partner. Everyone who has had a doula speaks very highly of them.

just took total control and told us both what to do. And the odd thing was that Flora is the only person I know who specified that she didn't want to have a water birth who ended up having one. The midwife came in and said, 'We have a water birthing facility free,' and the doula said, 'Right, we're going to have it,' and dragged her off and made her sit in it. Because usually it's the other way round, isn't it? People who want water births always end up having epidurals and the rest.

Both births were at St Thomas's, and both rooms had views of the House of Commons, which was very nice. I remember going for a walk in the middle of the night, doing a loop over Westminster Bridge and Trafalgar Square and then back down and round, and looking up at the clouds, which were orange with reflected light, and thinking, I will look at this scene and I will look at clouds like this again, but everything will have changed.

CLIFF: I did not enjoy the fact that somebody you ostensibly like is going through all this pain. I don't know when it switched round so that fathers are now expected to be at the birth, as far as I can see just to be shouted at. Because I'd done the classes. I may not have paid attention at all the classes. But whenever I tried saying 'Breathe' I was always screamed at. I remember being very nervous. I think I took things to read, but couldn't concentrate, and I do remember discovering that the floor was very good for tap-dancing, and trying to calm myself and take my mind off it by doing little tap routines. For some inexplicable reason that did annoy my wife even more, and possibly the midwives as well. That's all I remember – I mean, that and the immense amount of blood, and not really under-

standing enough to know whether all the blood should have been there or not. I tried getting out of the room as much as possible ...

KARL: One of my most vivid memories is of having called a taxi, standing out on G—— Road at four o'clock in the morning in January, listening to the screams inside the front door, as Kirsty virtually gave birth on the staircase. We got her into the taxi and I began to realise that things were getting a bit serious when we got to Putney Bridge and the driver goes, 'Want me to jump the lights, guv'nor?' Ah yes, let's go for it. And we got to the hospital at about half past four, twenty to five, and it was horrible. The taxi driver let us out of the car and started making this Dickensian speech: 'Sir, madam, I should like to wish you the best of ...' And I am going, 'Yeah, look, here's a tenner, thanks mate, great, now can we just have a wheelchair here?' And we just went up in the lift, into the maternity suite, and out he came. Jolly lucky not to be born in the back of the taxi.

JEROME: The other thing we were told was, make sure you bring in a bottle of champagne for that important moment. It actually had been quite a difficult birth and quite gory and at the end of it, when the midwife was trying to clean up, I then said, 'We ought to open that champagne.' The midwife said, 'Fine, I'll have a glass.' I opened this champagne which went PHWWWWOOFFF all over the place, so I was quite popular for that as well. They had to clear that up on top of everything else. It was all just stuff I had read. These are the things you should do to have a fantastic birth experience. It was all drivel.

KARL: Now our third boy, four years later ... again, this was slightly cross-making. Again it was in the evening that we began to realise that something was happening, so I go out, get a taxi, and off we go to the hospital. And you know, third baby, it's going to be like shelling peas, boys, no problems here. And I'm thinking, that's all right, I might get home for breakfast. And the night began to unwind. And in the end there was a snag ... there weren't enough midwives on duty. The one assigned to us kept disappearing. And all of a sudden there was a problem with the baby: the cord had got stuck around his leg. And suddenly there are four doctors ... God knows why, but I had great confidence in the medical profession, so even then I wasn't distressed by this. Obviously half of me was deeply involved and a part of all this, and the other half was thinking, if I get home by breakfast I might be able to do some work at about midday. It all worked out in the end of course. She couldn't walk for three days afterwards. But he was a big boy. He was 9lb 10oz. Monster baby.

BASIL: The plan for our first baby was straightforward enough. A water birth at home, attended by me, the best NHS homebirth midwife in the district and her assistant, a skilled birth helper (a trained obstetrician turned water birth guru), and her assistant. Gentle music, soft lighting, massage, minimal pain relief – gas and air – ending in a painful but smooth, swift and beautiful birth in the warm water of the pool. I, the tired but elated father, cutting the baby's cord when it stopped pulsating naturally. A tired, blissful mother cradling the baby in the pool.

The reality was more like Stalingrad. Witnessing a human

being suffering 22 hours of excruciating pain. The birth helper disagreeing with the midwife and, aside, trying to persuade me to make a decision in her favour. Me vaguely thinking, Surely you're the fucking expert? but too stupidly polite (and bewildered and headfucked after two sleepless nights) to articulate it. The midwife reluctant to admit defeat when it must have been obvious that T had a head the size of an elephant and was STUCK, rhymes with FUCK. Running out of gas and air. The midwife driving off to get some. My wife on all fours in the back of the birth helper's car. The birth helper reluctant to exceed the 30 mph limit on the mile drive to the hospital. Me telling her I think the police might understand in this instance. The birth helper reluctant to park by the admissions door in the spot reserved for emergency vehicles. Me, cross-eyed and almost speechless with exhaustion, pointing out that if this car isn't an ambulance I don't know what is. The admissions doctor writing 'distressed and abusive' in my wife's admission notes. The absence of staff on the bank holiday weekend. My wife howling for That Fucking Epidural Now as we wait for the anaesthetist. The camp and sniffy anaesthetist who is damned if anything is going to make him hurry casually getting his stuff ready with no apparent signs of urgency and chatting amiably to the birth helper, who turns out to be an old friend of his, over the slumped figure of my wife. Hearing him say to the birth helper, 'We must have lunch sometime.' Hearing my wife, at this, expressing her opinion of doctors with a crazed but impressively articulate torrent of swearwords. Witnessing her on the trolley being wheeled into the arc lights and alien machinery of the operating theatre. Seeing green curtains go up around her abdomen while the registrar and crew get ready. Sitting at my wife's head talking her through our favourite walk in Crete to distract her while her whole body is rocked from side to side by the unspeakable carnage being performed three feet away. Feeling my wife rebound as the baby is wrenched out. Glimpsing the still-pulsating cord being sliced through at once as the pinkish-blueish-greyish baby is whisked off, barely seen, to another part of the room. Standing and glancing over the curtain and seeing what looks like something in the back of a butcher's shop. Sitting down very hastily. Hearing the anaesthetist impatiently say, 'Please everyone, can we get this one finished?' as my wife, now utterly gaga from exhaustion, trauma and a bucket of chemicals, lapses into full-blown Tourette's syndrome. Hearing the baby cry for the first time, somewhere among strangers and machines. Being presented with the baby by a smiling female doctor. Almost too tired for joy, tearful but sensing that I had to keep it together a little bit longer. Pledging the strange blotchy little creature all my care and love forever. My wife, finally stitched up, rather reluctantly holding the ten-pound big-headed monster that has sent her to the depths of hell and not quite back. Saying goodnight to mother and sleeping baby in a side ward at about eleven at night, 48 hours after the first pre-labour cramps, about 22 hours after the onset of the real thing. Walking home with bag of chips. Thinking Jesus Christ, I'm a dad.

IVAN: When the time came for W to be born, a doctor came in, a Dr B——, I'll never forget his name. Of course, having gone to NCT, we had our birth plan, and we knew basically what was going on, and the one thing she had said to the doctor was, I don't want to be cut, I want to tear. And as W was coming out, the next thing I knew was, there was an arc of blood shooting out across the delivery room, because this bastard had whipped out a scalpel and cut her, to make the birth easier – basically for himself, which is what doctors tend to do. On top of that, when he stitched her up, he cocked it up. She spent six months after the birth in a lot of pain and discomfort. Eventually she had to go to another hospital to have an operation to put it right again. Someone had to cut her open again, then stitch her up again. But this doctor, Dr B——, as he was stitching her up, he uttered the immortal words: 'One for the husband.' Which meant he was going to stitch her up a little bit tighter. It's 16 years ago, but I would love to hit that guy in the face, even now.

To get to the good part – and I think this is peculiar to the first one – when W was finally born and I saw him there, that was the most amazing experience of my life. I always describe it as the Frankenstein moment, because the first feeling was this sudden rush of blood to the head, and you think, my God, we've created life. And I felt immensely powerful. And immediately afterwards you feel incredibly humble, because you think, oh my God, look at this little thing down there. I wept. Imogen wept. It was the single greatest moment of my life.

LESTER: After our scanning experience in one of Prague's two maternity hospitals, we booked into the other one for the big day. All seemed well. There was even an English-speaking nurse to help us so we wouldn't have to rely on our Czech.

The first hurdle was our son's unwillingness to be born. The due date came and went. Lilith guzzled beer hoping to get him drunk and trick him into dropping down. She went on long bumpy tram rides over the cobbled streets of the Old Town, but nothing would shift him. He would have to be induced.

On the big day we travelled to the hospital in style, catching one last tram in the hope of some action. Lilith bemused the polite Praguers by refusing every offer of a seat. Once at the hospital, she was installed in a waiting room and told that our English-speaking nurse was off sick. I was shooed off to work. I left Lilith in fine form loudly practising the Czech for 'When do I get the drugs?'

Two hours later I managed to dodge the guards and track Lilith down. By this time she had been moved to a delivery room, having been given the injection to start the induction. 'When do I get the drugs?' Lilith wailed at me as I entered. To judge from her physical appearance she had been getting the drugs on a daily basis for the previous ten years. The healthy young wife I had left two hours previously now looked like Anita Pallenberg going cold turkey.

Time for me to leap into action. Having tracked down a nurse, I rattled through my recently-learnt pain relief vocabulary, moving fluently from epidurals to anaesthetic to paracetamol. 'No drugs now. Drugs later,' came the reply over a departing shoulder.

By this time Lilith was vomiting liberally and was unable to stand up, sit down or do much other than lie in a heap on the floor. After much experimentation, we finally discovered that if Lilith lay on top of me on the bed with her full body weight bearing down on my right shoulder, she was able to stop vomiting and give her full attention to screaming.

In this way the next ten hours passed. Every so often a nurse popped in to see how we were getting on. She would let us know how many Czech women had successfully given birth since her last visit, tut at our lack of progress and chant 'No drugs now. Drugs later,' before leaving. The only variation in this routine was when after six hours the nurse told us, 'No drugs now. The anaesthetist, he go home,' before she exited the room, oblivious to the storm of English abuse following her out of the door.

Finally the nurse, despairing of any action, summoned a doctor. He took one look at what was left of Lilith and told me in good English, 'Your wife can't have any drugs now, the anaesthetist has gone home. Perhaps I can find some gas for her.' I hoped he meant oxygen.

Suddenly the room became crowded. Hundreds of midwives appeared. Apparently the hospital was running a training course and no one wanted to miss out on the chance to witness a foreigner giving birth. They formed a line at the end of the bed, in their white trousers and jackets looking bizarrely like a row of slip fielders. The head nurse was even holding a towel over her hands, making her look exactly like a wicketkeeper, I thought. I began to realise that I was in serious need of a drink.

Progress was cricket-like, too. Nothing happened. Our baby just refused to move. Lilith and the doctor exchanged pleasantries. 'Push Missis,' he requested. 'I am fucking pushing,' Lilith assured him, the veins popping on her forehead. After a fruitless half hour, the doctor decided to take the bull by the horns. If nature couldn't shift our son, perhaps brute force would. To this end, he lay on Lilith's stomach and pushed. Hard.

Throughout her pregnancy Lilith had spent hours staring worriedly at my head. It is fair to say that I take a generous size in hats. Her worries were about to prove well founded.

Suddenly there was a hundred per cent increase in the number of people in the room screaming. Forced rudely into the world, our son joined Lilith in her chorus of disapproval. The head midwife held him up triumphantly. 'How weird,' I thought to myself, 'he's got large purple feet.' The midwife then passed him down the line of waiting midwives in a manner that immediately made me think of a scrum-half passing out the ball to the wings. I half expected the final midwife to charge off with our baby and drop him between two imaginary posts. I was now desperate for a drink.

The doctor handed me our son. 'Congratulations, you have a son,' he told me, pointlessly. Turning to my wife, he smiled and said, 'I'm afraid your vagina has been destroyed,' while reaching for his needle and thread. It was a memorable end to a memorable day.

Lilith was kept in hospital for eleven days while she recovered from the joys of childbirth Czech-style. It took considerably longer for her to be fully fit again.

Our son is an only child.

10
new life

The baby is born, and a new life begins. Actually, that's not quite accurate: three new lives begin. You will probably want to harm anyone who tells you that things will never be the same again, although they speak the truth. Just how different your life will be we shall address in the next few chapters. The learning curve is steep, but you should be able to negotiate it with crampons and a good strong harness. As it happens, mountaineering and childrearing have much in common: they are not for the faint-hearted and there's a lot of expensive equipment to buy. And amazingly, some people do them both for fun.

The baby is born, and it's got your nose. Folk wisdom tells us that the first child will look more like the father than the mother – this is nature's way of reassuring him that he is indeed the father. However much you trust your partner, however carefully you have kept her locked up in a dungeon wearing a chastity belt for the past five years, your first instinct as a new father will be to check that the baby looks like you. This is not as daft as it sounds. Around a tenth of British babies, it is thought, do not have the father everyone thinks they have. And yet a hundred per cent of new fathers are told by relatives and friends, 'He/she's got your nose.' People want to believe. But more than that, they want *you* to believe – even if the evidence (baby is the wrong colour, or has strange pointy ears) suggests otherwise.

Here are a few more thoughts that will pour unbidden into your exhausted mind:

- 'It's so small.'
- 'It's so big.'
- 'How on earth did it get out of there?'

The sheer oddness of birth hits everyone. This is a routine, daily occurrence, but when you see it for yourself, it seems weird, startling, miraculous. Hold the baby in your arms, if you dare. This tiny little person, a stranger to everyone, has emerged fully formed with an operating personality and two big eyes, which it is now probably training on its mother's breasts. As well as being very small, it is also huge, having somehow worked its way down the birth canal with the minimum of assistance. All this is almost too much to take in at once, which is why all you can think at the moment is: I'd better not drop it.

This, too, is normal. All new fathers are obsessed with not dropping the baby. I have never seen this mentioned in any of the books, but it's our overwhelming concern. Most of us have never held a newborn baby before. Most of us have fled the house rather than hold a newborn baby. But you can't avoid holding your own.

So what if you do drop it? First, you will establish whether or not it bounces. As it happens, small babies are remarkably resilient. There are countless tales of newborns falling great heights and suffering little more than minor bruising. Not that you should test this out. Babies don't like being used as projectiles and, indeed, there are laws against it. So try not to drop your baby – in much the same way that you don't drop newspapers, cups of tea and bottles of milk every day of your life.

Because now you'll be holding the baby every day of your life as well.

Luckily, small babies don't do a huge amount. Holding them is very easy. The big surprise is how floppy they are. Newborn babies have 360 bones (adults have just 206). But there's no strength there yet. The neck muscles are noticeably non-functional: you'll probably have to hold the baby's body with one hand and its head with the other. With practice – i.e. in about half an hour – you will be able to hold the baby in the crook of one arm, leaving one hand free to operate heavy machinery. For the moment, get comfortable, breathe normally, relax, and look baby in the eyes. If baby is eight to ten inches from your face, he/she will be able to see you and, indeed, smell you, and so will get to know you in the most visceral ways possible. Chances are that after a 16-hour labour you won't smell too great. But baby won't mind. If he/she starts crying it's because something else is wrong, not because Daddy stinks like a baboon. Parents' personal hygiene is remarkably low on their list of priorities.

This can be another good moment for the father. The mother is still groaning with exhaustion, and may be having her various parts sewn back together. Holding your new baby, you may (according to one of the books) 'experience a wave of euphoria' – or, if we are going to be candid, a sense of how incredibly clever you are. And why not? This is your achievement as much as hers, and yet she has had to do all the work. We read of women who have penis envy, but have you ever heard of a man who has womb envy? Despite the fact that you have done nothing these nine months, the baby is 50 per cent you. Some mothers never forgive the father for this. If the relationship goes wrong, some mothers never forgive the children either, which is huge fun for everyone concerned, as you can imagine.

It may be, of course, that you do not experience a wave of euphoria at the first sight of your baby, or anything like it. Instead, you may feel miserable or furious, or just numb. Many men do. It is allowed. But probably best to keep it to yourself for now.

NEWBORN BABIES: A USER'S GUIDE

I'm assuming at this point that the baby is in reasonable health. It's relatively easy to tell whether or not this is the case. If it isn't, hospital staff will be swarming around like bees. If it is, they will already have disappeared for a cup of tea and the two of you (or three, if there's a birth partner) will be left in the delivery room wondering what you are supposed to do next. As during pregnancy, there are 1,001 things that *can* go wrong, but very few that are likely to go wrong. Given a little luck, you and your partner should have nothing more to show for all this effort than an empty room and a small baby. Here are a few of that baby's salient features:

- **Weight.** As in adults and children, amazing variations in size and weight are standard. Anything between 5lb 8oz and 9lb 12oz is 'within normal parameters', as they say on Star Trek. Be aware that if the baby weighs over 9lb, you are obliged by all known laws of baby etiquette to call it 'a whopper'.

- **It looks a bit battered.** So would you if you had just been through that. There may be some bruises, and dried blood, and the head may seem elongated, even if ventouse hasn't been used. It's nothing to worry about.

- **Skin.** If the baby is a little early or even if it's bang on time, it may be covered with white greasy stuff called vernix, and will look as though it's ready to swim the English Channel. Inside the womb vernix (technically, *vernix caseosa*, which is Latin for 'cheesy varnish') waterproofs the skin against the amniotic fluid, as well as protecting the foetus against bumps and scrapes. You really don't want to know what it's made of[8], but it does the job until scraped off by midwives wearing huge rubber gloves.[9]

---

8. Fatty material and dead skin cells.
9. Apparently it makes fantastic skin cream. Pop it in a little pot and you could probably sell it for 20 quid.

Overdue babies, by contrast, may have dry or flaky skin, and look a little prune-like. Many babies have a yellowish tinge. This is jaundice, and very common. All it means is that the liver isn't yet up to speed. It soon sorts itself out, although the suspicion that your beautiful new baby has been coloured in with felt pen may be hard to dispel.

- **Hair.** Some babies are bald. Some have a shock of hair. Premature babies sometimes have downy body hair called lanugo, which can be a different sort of shock. Immediate response: have we given birth to a chimp? But it falls out very quickly, as it would have done in the womb if the baby had gone to full term. (Lanugo literally means 'wool', and is also the technical term for the fuzz on a peach.) The head hair should also fall out in the first three months and may grow back in a different colour. Not unlike Sir Elton John's.

- **Skull.** At birth the baby's head may seem disproportionately large. (In fact it's the eyes that are disproportionately largest, and will have to grow the least between now and adulthood.) Slightly more disturbingly, the skull bones will be soft, which is how the head can change shape during birth and in the immediate aftermath. The skullbones won't fuse completely for several months. In the meantime there's a soft spot on top popularly known as the fontanelle (which is actually the name of the membrane that covers it). It's roughly diamond shaped, and you should be able to see a pulse beating there. Nothing more vividly represents the absolute vulnerability of the newborn.

- **Genitals.** Are they vast and a bit purple? If so, it's nothing to do with you. Pregnancy hormones, not genetics, make them that way. They will revert to normal size within a few days. But take a few photos first to impress gullible non-parents.

- **Hearing.** Baby's sight may not yet be 20/20, but he/she has been listening to you and your partner arguing for nine months now, and recognises your voices. Newborns often respond to the sounds of pleasure in their parents' voices, which can be amazingly gratifying. Here at last is someone who doesn't mind when you drone on and on about nothing in particular, as long as you sound reasonably cheerful while doing it. They love it when you sing and say silly nursery rhymes. And when you shout or argue, they will probably cry.

- **Umbilical cord.** The stump should dry up and shrivel within a couple of days. Then, before the first week is up, the midwife should remove the clamp. Then the whole thing should drop off within another few days. Women don't seem to worry about this, but men, who live in fear of having things dry up, shrivel and drop off, can take it all very personally.

THE FIRST BREASTFEED

Baby is no fool: no sooner is it out in the world, breathing dank British air, than it starts to get peckish. Fortunately there are two readily available sources of nourishment to hand. Clamping baby to the mother's breast within an hour of birth increases the chance that baby will eventually breastfeed successfully. Some babies take to the breast immediately, and the milk gushes out, in which case, great. Other mothers and/or babies find it all the most terrible struggle. None of this has much to do with you, the father. This is when some men start to feel excluded from things, when the unbreachable bond between mother and baby first forms. But breastfeeding is a good thing, even for the cast-aside dad. Encourage it at all costs. Here's why.

Breast milk, as we will come to know and sniff and even taste it, does not kick in until three or four days after the birth. Baby's first feed will be a substance called colostrum, a sort of milky hors d'oeuvre high in protein and stuffed with important anti-bodies that will protect baby from infections and boost the immune system. Having watched two babies grow to toddler-hood on breast milk, I have come to believe that breastfeeding is, in its way, even more miraculous than the birth process. Everything baby needs in its first six months is in those two mighty mounds. It's psychologically healthy for the baby, and also for the mother: endorphins start to flow as she feeds, relax-ing her and even cheering her up, if she needs cheering. The milk is easy to digest; it's always there; it's the right temperature; it's sterile; it's full of minerals and vitamins and other good things. Breastfeeding helps burn off the mother's exciting new fat reserves. Babies have fewer nappy rashes and their shit does-n't smell as bad. And best of all? No bottle feeds for Daddy in the middle of the night. Hallelujah and praise the Lord: this is indeed a miracle. But more of this later.

THE BRINGER OF GLAD TIDINGS

As mother and baby bond, and you begin to think seriously about sitting down and reading the paper, it's time for your next job: calling the relatives.

Mobile phones are banned in hospitals. You must use the public phones that line most corridors. Did you remember to bring lots of pound coins? And did you spend them all on crisps and mouldering Bounty bars during labour? Change machines, though a marvellous idea, wouldn't survive a night in most hospitals. Maybe there should be the maternity ward equivalents of ticket touts hanging around in trilbys, with unlit fags dangling from their thin lips, offering you change for a fiver at usurious rates. Do not ask hospital staff for change. They have already been asked eleven times since they came on shift. Even if they don't assault you, they may choose to mishear you and pocket the note as a tip.

Among all the stuff you packed for labour (most of it unused and not even thought about) will be a list of people to call which your partner compiled several weeks ago when she felt the first false twinge. The list is usually graded in strict priority: her parents; her siblings; her best friend; her other close friends; her former workmates; her best friend from school she hasn't seen for years; local tradesmen; random people off the street; your parents, friends, etc. It's just because she is jealous. Calling everyone with the good news is much more fun than what she has just gone through. Everyone will be delighted to hear from you. You can even milk the situation a bit by pretending you are ringing about something else and then springing the good news on them when they are least expecting it. Cruel, but fun. Make sure you have all these vital pieces of information to hand:

- sex of baby;
- weight in pounds and ounces of new baby (groceries may be measured in kilos, babies are not):
- length of labour in hours and minutes;
- colour of hair (if any);
- confirmation that baby has your nose/ears/distinguished forehead.

And try and edit out the following:

- quantity of blood and gore witnessed during the long hours of horror;
- current resemblance of partner's birth canal to four-lane bypass;
- own resemblance to Albert Steptoe with bad hangover.

For you it may be grim reality, but for everyone else it's a beautiful fantasy. Try and keep it that way if you want decent presents.

> *CLIFF: I remember thinking it was incredibly ugly. I still see photos of my firstborn now and other people say, 'Isn't he sweet?' and I think, well, no, sorry. I can't say I bonded immediately with what he looked like because he was just staggeringly ugly – although I dislike all babies, so I didn't really know what to compare it to.*

WHAT IF YOUR BABY IS UGLY?

There is a school of thought that would suggest that all babies are ugly. And it's true that a remarkable number look like Sir Winston Churchill in his later, dribblier years. Occasionally a couple will have a truly hideous baby. It's more likely if they look like gargoyles themselves, but even airbrushed celebrities have suffered this fate, for there is surprisingly little correlation between ugliness at birth and the more profound uglinesses of adulthood. Several outstandingly hideous babies I have known have become extremely presentable children – although it often goes wrong in adolescence, like so much else. Even the killer combination of weak chin and big flappy ears can sometimes be overcome, and not just by surgery.

But whether or not the baby is ugly doesn't matter that much. What really matters is whether or not *you* think it's ugly. Her friends and everybody's relatives will coo anyway. Your friends will want to keep away from it however gorgeous it is. The beauty or otherwise of your baby is your concern, and yours only. And I mean you, the father, because the mother will think it's the prettiest baby ever born even if it looks like John Prescott. She is programmed to believe this. Whereas you will probably look down at your firstborn and think … it's a baby. (You may be programmed to think this too. After all, biologically you have done your job, and as a healthy, active male of species *homo sapiens* you should now be looking for someone else to impregnate. Apparently, good-looking midwives are always being hit upon by new dads. 'Like being chained to an idiot …')

So don't worry if your baby is ugly. You will learn to love it. Or maybe not.

'SPECIAL CARE'

Now there's a euphemism to chill the blood. Around ten per cent of newborns require 'special care' after birth and are therefore shifted off to the Special Care Baby Unit. This includes premature babies (those born before 37 weeks) and babies weighing less than 5lb 8oz (whether premature or not), as well as babies who have picked up infections or struggled with breathing during birth. There's nothing wrong, in short, that can't be fixed with a short spell in an incubator, where baby can be monitored and fed intravenously and brought gently into the world. It's worth noting here that infant mortality these days is very low – down to six per 1,000 births. (Half of these are still-births.) In 1850, in England and Wales, around 150 of every 1,000 babies died within the first month – a figure that changed little over the following 50 years. Since then, though, the rate has consistently declined, apart from a brief blip during World War Two. In 1960 it was 20 per 1,000, so huge advances have been made even in the past few years. Bear in mind that around 70 of every 1,000 newborns weigh less than 5lb 8oz, which makes you realise that however tiny and underfed and plain unwell your little baby may look, pure probability is in your favour. 40 years ago twelve per cent of low birth weight babies died in the first month. Now it's around four per cent. There are some babies who are never going to survive. But the vast majority of the rest will pull through.

So if your baby is put in an incubator, the first thing is not to panic.

Naturally you will be worried. Possibly even bricking yourself with terror. After the ghastliness of the birth, an incubator may feel like the last straw. But be aware that for the mother it will be even worse. Miriam Stoppard in *The New Parent* says it's like losing a limb. The baby should be lying in its mother's arms, not under a plastic cover like an old sandwich. Rationally, you know that unless the baby is seriously ill, it probably will be lying in its mother's arms within a few days, maybe sooner. But your considerable experience watching bad hospital dramas on TV still leads you to fear the worst. Try and forget all that. Be strong and Clint-like. And keep your fingers crossed.

THE MATERNITY WARD

If 'special care' isn't required, we move instead to the female stronghold that is the maternity ward. You thought you felt uncomfortable and out of place in the delivery room? Think again. Compared to the maternity ward, the delivery room was like an old man's pub just before closing time. Though at least partly responsible for making these bright new babies, the few males who pass through the swing doors are given filthy glares by nurses, mothers, grandmothers and all the other 793 unidentifiable female relatives of someone or other who are milling around slightly menacingly. As I understand it, it's because they think we are going to stay five minutes and then run away, whereas what they'd like us to do is hang around for four hours cooing at the baby, fetching people cups of tea and telling the female relatives how much weight they have lost. But, of course, we stay five minutes and then run away, because the atmosphere there is so intimidating. Another chicken-and-egg argument. Somewhere in all this, of course, are your partner and your baby, but they may both be too out of it to care.

40 or so years ago, when I was born, my mother stayed in hospital for three weeks convalescing, even though there was nothing wrong with her. Nowadays the shortage of maternity beds is so fierce, and the chances of catching superbugs so high, that in some hospitals they have barely delivered the baby before they are giving you directions to the bus stop. Twenty-four hours of in-hospital care is fairly standard, 48 hours a miraculous gift from a generous management. There's one obvious advantage to all this rush and bluster, which is that mother

and baby will ingest the absolute minimum amount of hospital food. But the quick turnaround does place a lot of pressure on Exhausted New Dad. You may have had it in mind to go home and get 20 hours' sleep to make up for all the stresses of the past few days. In addition, you may have heard of the legend of Wetting The Baby's Head, which requires father to go to the pub with his friends who will buy him drinks for as long as he promises never to show them the video footage of the birth. Sleep, then drink; or drink, then sleep; either would be just about perfect. And both are impossible. The twenty-first-century hospital birth allows no time for anything. Before you can think of a good reason to object, you will be driving them back to the sty of your home, hoping that your partner, whose stitches may still be a bit tender, doesn't haemorrhage all over the back seat of the car. Don't laugh: I'm told the stains are impossible to get out.

11

the importance of being ernest (or ernestina)

They will ask you how much it weighs, whether the labour was long or short, how the mother is doing, does it have your eyes. And then, almost as an afterthought, they will ask the killer question. 'Have you thought of any names yet?'

My, have you thought of some names yet.

While the baby is still unborn, most parents will give it a temporary name, which may or may not be a joke. Two good friends of mine threatened throughout their pregnancy to burden their forthcoming daughter with the name 'Yoda', partly to amuse their friends but mainly to annoy their parents. They called her something else in the end, of course. Even so, in my four-year-old's class at kindergarten, there was a Luke, there was an Obe (pronounced Obi) and there was a Lya (nearly pronounced Leia).

I suggested changing our daughter's name to Grand Moff Tarkin to help her to fit in better. For strange things have happened to children's names over the past few years. Blame the parents of Kylie Minogue, of Beyoncé Knowles, and of all those actors called Ethan. For a while I suspected that it was a London thing, and that elsewhere in the country parents were still calling their little ones sensible things like John and Susan. But no. Given the freedom to choose anything, parents have started to choose anything, whether it is a recognised name or not. In 2002, 66 newborn babies were named Chardonnay. That includes 14 whose parents spelled it with only one 'n'. None of these parents seem to have worked out that the name was given to a character in 'Footballers' Wives' as a JOKE. Maybe the trend will spread, and small boys will soon be named Merlot, or Pinot Noir.

Celebrities, as so often, are the true culprits. When Bob Geldof and Paula Yates called their children Pixie, Fifi Trixibelle and Peaches in the 1980s, everyone laughed. Now they would probably be praised for their restraint. It's hard enough for children of successful parents to make their own way in the world, without being named after soft fruit or household pets. And yet celebrities continue to give their children the silliest names:

POOR BENIGHTED CHILDREN	IDIOT PARENT(S)
Lennon	Liam Gallagher & Patsy Kensit
Jaden Gil	Steffi Graf & André Agassi
Sailor Lee	Christie Brinkley
Phoenix Chi	Mel B out of the Spice Girls

Child	Parent(s)
Apple	Gwyneth Paltrow & Chris Martin
Rumer Glenn & Scout Marue	Bruce Willis & Demi Moore
Denim	Toni Braxton
Moon Unit, Dweezil & Diva	Frank Zappa
Elijah Blue & Chastity Sun	Cher
Happy	Macy Gray
Brooklyn (girl)	Donna Summer
Brooklyn & Romeo (boys)	Victoria & David Beckham
Memphis Eve & Elijah Bob Patricius Guggi Q	Bono
Justice	Steven Seagal
Ocean & Sonnet	Forest Whitaker
Speck Wildhorse	John Cougar Mellencamp

They get their revenge in the end. Keith Richards's daughter was christened Dandelion, and now calls herself Angela. David Bowie's son was christened Zowie and now calls himself Joe. What they call their fathers is anyone's guess.

How much simpler it used to be, and not just in the UK. Until 1970 the names of French children had to be chosen from an approved list issued by the Ministry of the Interior. Jean-Paul or Jean-Luc – no problem. But Paul-Jean or Luc-Jean – forget it. Foreign names were a particular no-no. It's pleasing to think that, somewhere in the dark and forgotten recesses of the French penal system, there may still be men and women chained to walls who once dared to call their children Mario or Dave.

So, what you do call your little precious? Pocket-sized paperbacks of Babies' Names will offer several hundred to choose from, but once you have discounted the ones that sound ridiculous, the ones everyone else seems to have, the ones you can't use because you have always hated someone with that name, the annoying Irish ones no one knows how to spell, the ones that recall previous boyfriends and girlfriends and husbands and wives, the ones that sound poncy or namby or thuggish or dim, the ones so out of fashion no one will ever use them again, and Dave, that doesn't leave an awful lot. Indeed, if you can stretch to a short list of six you will be doing well. Some parents just end up with 'Emily', remember they have a boy, and have to start again from scratch.[10]

The crucial thing, as you compile your shortlist, is that the name should pass the Playground Test. In two or three years' time you will be in a playground with your infant, who won't be doing what it's told. And you will have to shout, 'Aurora, stop doing that!' And people will snigger or snort. One or two will have coughing fits. Aurora is one of several names that fail the Playground Test. So do Nigella, LaToya and Arundhati (if you're Scottish). For boys, try and avoid Rock, Clarence, Reginald and Speck Wildhorse. For fear of offending too many readers, I shall go no further, but you know what I am talking about.

More problematic, I'm afraid, are the vagaries of fashion. Names drift in and out, dulled by familiarity and then

---

10. An unusual surname could reduce your options yet further. My girlfriend's cousin recently spoke to someone on the phone called Allan Key. As he said, it's like being called Screwdriver and naming your child Philip.

rediscovered by new generations of desperate parents. I have known an awful lot of Simons and Stephens and Sarahs and Lucys in my life – of these, only Lucy still seems to have any currency. A few years ago, in my sheltered corner of north London, there was a sudden surge of Felixes. Oliver has been and gone and come back, and may have gone again, for all I know. There are truckloads of Finlays, and more Phoebes than can ever have been the plan. We know several Albies and Alfies, but no little Nigels. Are there any little Nigels? Anywhere?

A lot of this is obviously to do with class and geography – there will be areas of the country where Tim is a more manageable name than Kevin, and vice versa. Americans complicate matters unnecessarily by insisting that Robin is a girl's name, and by not knowing that Chelsea is a football team. Do not be distracted. With luck and deep thought you may yet think of a name that isn't too ridiculous and hasn't been nabbed by someone else. Only recently, a friend told me with pride that his newborn nephew was going to be called Monty. It was the pride of a man who knew that there was no glut of Montys, that there might indeed be a shortage of Montys, even an absence of Montys. My daughter told him there was one in her class. His face fell with a clump.

But remember this. As you edge towards making your minds up, be aware that this child will carry its name for life, and will therefore be identified and even judged by these syllables that you will have decided on in only a couple of days when both of you were exhausted and slightly mad. Put it this way: Arbuthnot and Iolanthe might seem like a good idea right now, but they never will again, until the end of time.

12
stuff

IVAN: Nothing prepares you for the complete seismic change in your life that occurs when your child is born. Oh, it'll be wonderful. You don't think about it too much. And then suddenly you start seeing the money going out of your account on prams and pushchairs and all the rest of it. I remember that W cost us a thousand pounds before he was even born, and that was just on baby clothes and ridiculous prams and pushchairs. The pram I think we used three times before it was sold on, at some boot sale or something. Silver Cross pram. The most ridiculous piece of machinery ever invented. And things like baby chairs for cars and stuff. It's an expensive business.

Before baby, your home probably felt quite comfortably sized, with room enough for most of the things and people you wished to fit into it. After baby, Blenheim Palace would seem cramped. As you bring home mother-and-baby for the first time – they come as a package now – you will realise not only how little space you now have for them, but how little you will have for all the stuff you are going to have to buy in the coming days, months and years. Stuff. It's only a little word. In the old days it meant nice things, like cameras and hi-fi equipment and cars and enormous TVs. Anything that needed batteries. Anything that could be plugged in. And absolutely anything that came with a remote control.

But now you are a father, and you are looking at a different kind of stuff. You can still buy all that electrical equipment, if you are a multi-millionaire and you tell your partner you inherited it from a recently deceased aunt who had worked at Dixons. Otherwise your shopping hours will now be dedicated to the purchase of stuff for your baby. This, as everyone knows, costs a fortune. It is frequently suggested in newspapers, which have usually got the figure from other newspapers, that the cost of looking after a child from 0 to 18 years is upwards of £250,000. Or, if you choose the special bargain rate, four kids for a million. We'll throw in the first nappy for free. Can't say fairer than that, can we?

New fathers whose chests started palpitating towards the end of the last paragraph and have since been rushed to hospital will therefore not find out that this £250,000 figure seems to have been chosen completely at random. (When broken down into constituent expenses it often includes such necessities as twelve years of independent schooling and a new car on Junior's seventeenth birthday.) The real cost of childhood can be very much lower. And there are what economists call opportunity costs to bring into the equation. If you are staying at home for 15 or 20 years looking after children instead of going out and whooping it up at costly nightspots, you could save a lot of money. Good grief, if you cut down on taxis, sport and holidays you might even clear a profit. You will be fat and miserable, but you won't necessarily be poor.

Even so, the entry fee is high. There is a lot of stuff you need to have, and soon. The sheer quantity of infant-related paraphernalia takes the breath away, especially when you are carrying it all. Before Arbuthnot or Iolanthe have issued their first meconium poo, you will need to at least think about acquiring all of the following:

- Somewhere for baby to sleep. Most of the books recommend buying a Moses basket. This is a conveniently baby-shaped basket which comes with a sheet lining and has handles so you can carry it from room to room. Baby can sleep there during the day and during the night as well. Only problem: with a wooden stand thrown in, Moses baskets cost about £50. A ridiculous expense for a piece of equipment you won't need in a couple of months. Does anyone you know have one lying around the house? That they would be only too happy to lend or give you at no cost to you at all?

- A pushchair or pram. It's said that no one pushes prams any more, other than the very rich, who know a status symbol when they see one. But I'm not sure about this. I suspect some new parents buy prams because they think that's what you are supposed to buy, not realising that within two or three months they won't need it any more for anything. Most parenthood books now warn you away from prams, because they are so expensive, and because they are awkward: it's marginally easier to swim the English Channel than get a pram on a bus. Nonetheless, tiny babies do like a pram. Its flat surface is more comfortable, which means Junior is more likely to fall asleep and less likely to cry, both of which are good. So you have a few options. You could forget the pram entirely and go straight for the pushchair. Brutal, but cost effective. Or you could buy one of those pram-cum-pushchair convertibles, which are fun to tinker with, although like sofa beds, never quite as comfortable as the salesman will have you believe. Or you can find someone else who has bought a pram and doesn't need it any more. They will be desperate to get rid of it, because it takes up so much space. Offer to take it off their hands, and worry about pushchairs later.

- Nappies. A newborn baby needs its nappy changed up to 60 times a week. In the past, scary-sounding 'terry' nappies were the only option: you could use them again and again but your entire supply of them had to be boiled clean twice a day. Thanks to Pampers, Huggies and the like, this is no longer necessary. Unfortunately the disposable nappies create problems of their own. One is their expense: quite simply, they cost more than you ever imagined possible. Then there is their effect on the environment. This may not be an issue you care about greatly, but there's no avoiding the simple, horrendous truth: that by the end of the century, shit- and piss-filled nappies will occupy landfill sites the size of Belgium. And that's just the ones the Belgians have used, so you can imagine how badly off the rest of us are. But the manufacturers know that we are all now too lazy and soft to go back to 'terry' nappies. Disposables will probably be your single greatest expense in the first two years. (More on this later.)

● Changing mat. This is just a plastic, padded rectangle with either Winnie the Pooh or Mickey Mouse plastered all over it, just as shit will be quite soon. It may not look much but this will save your furniture and carpets and maybe your sanity into the bargain. An essential purchase.

● Muslins. You can't have too many of these either. They are cloth squares, about the size of large handkerchiefs, and you will use them for mopping up all kinds of stuff (let's not worry about the details just yet). 'Muslin' is another word you never used, or even heard, before parenthood. Now, whenever you hear anyone mention muslins, you will know that they too are members of the club.

● A car seat. Essential if you drive, as it's illegal to transport a small baby in a car without one. They are removable, which is helpful if baby drops off, as you can then carry it around as it sleeps. Again there is no need to buy this if you can get it for free. Someone you know will have a car seat they no longer need. Taking it off their hands will only do them a favour. (Children usually graduate to a bigger car seat when they are about a year old. Don't be shy about asking parents of one-year-olds if they need their old car seat. They will already be trying to blag a booster seat from someone else.)

You will notice a theme creeping in here. All parents need

stuff, but who wants to buy it? There are people who must have everything new, every muslin, every last vest, and that's fine, because it means they are buying the stuff the rest of us will later 'borrow' from them. Most parents want to get rid of stuff they no longer need, to make room for stuff they are about to need. You may not know it, but out there are thousands of micro-networks of like-minded parents, all saving each other money by handing things on they no longer want. The system works because much of this stuff easily outlasts any one baby's need for it. For instance:

- A baby bath. You can't scrub Junior in your proper bath, or your backbone would drop out. (It's also too big and scary for many little ones.) Showers are good for novelty bath games but little else. So it's nice to have a dedicated baby bath. For newborns a washing-up bowl will do, but Junior will outgrow that in a fortnight or so. In the meantime, go on the scrounge. Baby baths take up nearly as much room as a pram. I have known parents who have wept with relief when someone offered to take their baby bath away.

- Bottles and sterilising equipment. Definitely try and scrounge this. Your baby may breastfeed for ever and go nowhere near a bottle, and you could have all that expensive equipment sitting on a shelf for several years. Or until another canny new parent offers to take it off your hands.

This feels good, doesn't it?

Every day I look in the mirror each morning and tell myself, 'I am a mothwallet. I am a mothwallet and I don't care who knows it.'

Some things you will have to buy. A good sturdy pushchair should give you years of uncomplaining service. Someone else's cranky, rattly old vehicle may collapse the first time you take it more than five minutes' walk away from your home. (As you stand there wondering what to do, baby will poo itself, rain will start pouring and spaceships full of lizard-like aliens will land and enslave all humanity.) But there is also a thriving second-hand market out there. Even if you can't get everything for nothing, you should be able to snap things up for far less than shop price. It warms my ventricles just to think about it.

Even so, some readers of this book might be unconvinced. Some readers might come to the conclusion that this is all a bit stingy. That at this vivid and unrepeatable time we should be embracing life, not haggling over it. Consider this story from the *Daily Star* in January 2004:

> Russell Crowe turned into the Dadiator after splashing out £50,000 on a cot for his son.
>
> The *Gladiator* star spent over £150,000 on stuff for his boy Charles's nursery.
>
> Russell has told friends: 'I want nothing but the best for my boy – whatever the cost. He's going to have the best and coolest nursery in Australia.'
>
> The cot is a 19th-century Scandinavian design with ornate carvings. Also on his shopping list were some bedside lamps,

> and a painting called 'Reflection Of A Boy' – worth £75,000 – for the nursery wall.
>
> A source said: 'Russell chose all the items himself. It's clear he has got a really good eye.'

Of course he has. Anyone who has that much money always does.

Where the mothwallet approach really pays off is in the acquisition of clothes. Your baby, whatever its size, shape and vomiting preferences, will go through outrageous quantities of clothes. The stuff you have bought for its birth won't fit in a few weeks. In the first year you can look forward to a complete turnover of wardrobe three or four times. Babies grow in the first year as they will never grow again. They are dedicated growing machines. To buy new clothes for each new stage ... well, just the thought of it brings me out in a sweat. And lots of people do it. They may have loads of money, or they have weighed up the options and decided it is worth renting out their orifices in order to pay for it. But it is a choice; it is not strictly necessary. When our daughter was born my friend Esther gave us a black bin liner full of baby clothes. 'What do we need with 38 vests?' said my girlfriend, with a broad grin, as she piled them up neatly. But not all of them were for newborns, and we used every one in the end. And then we passed them on to someone else.

The beauty of this is that most children's clothes are often of very good quality; they have to be, in order to persuade mad parents to pay that amount of money for them. It is quite possible to leave a baby clothes emporium with a handful of small bags that between them have cost £75, £100, name your price.

Obviously, it's lovely to have a few new clothes – but that is where presents come in. With luck your indulgent relatives will buy several minuscule outfits for Junior. With more luck they will buy outfits to fit him/her in six or nine months' time, when you are really feeling the pinch. And with most luck they will buy practical clothes – vests, babygros, cardigans, blankets, hats, coats, woolly booties. As opposed to expensive but essentially useless items – party dresses, crop tops, trainers, cufflinks, three-piece suits, anything that needs handwashing or anything with lots of buttons.

A quick note on poppers. You may have noticed over the years that most children's clothes are covered with poppers, and you may have assumed that these would be both fiddly and annoying. Absolutely not. Poppers are a glorious and magnificent invention, utterly unconnected to the political philosopher Karl Popper (1902–94), which I always thought was a shame. Most vests and babygros (a.k.a. 'romper suits') have poppers so positioned that you have almost instant access to the nappy area, allowing you to remove a humdinger of a turd before your eyes begin to water and your nasal passages inflame. If there were buttons where poppers should be, you'd be swearing and shouting, the baby would be crying, and before long Social Services would be at the door taking your child away forever. Italian clothes, for some reason, often come with buttons rather than poppers, which explains a great deal.

Oh, and zips are good too. We like zips. (Except when they catch.)

If indulgent friends and relatives don't buy you clothes for the baby, they will probably give you a soft toy. Before you became a dad, when you went into the houses of people with small children, you probably noticed that they all had 300,000 soft toys. And you thought, what spoilt little bastards, and what pitifully indulgent parents. And again you were wrong. More likely than not, every one of those soft toys was a present from someone. Parents rarely buy them. They don't need to. It's the default present for small children when your imagination fails you, much as candles are for grown-ups.

Mothwallets know all of these things, and they usually keep quiet about them, for fear of being revealed as mothwallets. Here are the Fundamental Laws of Mothwallet, and clever parents should memorise them all.

First Law: Try and get as much as you can free. Some parents will be gagging to give away their old stuff. Cultivate them. If necessary, throw yourselves on their mercy.

Second Law: If buying second-hand, the rules are the same as for cars: you are almost certain to be ripped off. For all you know, that bargain pushchair may have been welded together from two unconnected halves of pushchair. And don't bother kicking the wheels. They saw you coming, my son.

Third Law: Never buy soft toys. Especially pink ones.

13
it's alive

'If you desire to drain to the dregs the fullest cup of scorn and hatred that fellow human beings can pour out for you, let a young mother hear you call her dear baby "it".' Jerome K. Jerome, 'On Babies' (1886)

It's lying in its crib, staring up at you. Staring hard. Not blinking. And thinking, 'You're a bit of an arse, aren't you?'

No it's not. That's just your imagination. Your brand new baby is capable of few thoughts more coherent than 'I'm hungry', 'I'm tired', 'I'm uncomfortable' and 'I'm bored'. Or the one he/she is thinking now, which is almost certainly 'I recognise you. You're that bloke.'

But the stare of a newborn baby cuts through its parents' defences like a razor through ricepaper. It seems to be able to see deep into your innermost soul, and it doesn't like what it sees there.

Put it down to tiredness or shock. Few new mothers seem to have this sort of reaction, but several new fathers have told me about it, later when drunk. They talk of the baby's devilish half-smile, of its unflinching gaze, of its seeming to know. 'Know what?' I say, fascinated. But the new father doesn't reply. He doesn't want me to know as well. He just stares into his drink and contemplates his fate.

What he probably doesn't know is that the devilish half-smile is a reflex, one of several you will be able to spot if you look close enough. The reflex smile (or 'pre-smile') has been seen in babies as young as three days old. It's a fleeting thing – gone before you have seen it, usually – and it disappears completely after a month, but it can seriously fuel fatherly paranoia, especially if you are finding the bonding process difficult. Drunks and the deranged shout 'Who are you looking at?' to anyone they pass – this is the new parent's equivalent. The reflex smile, I should add, is entirely meaningless.

The first few days of a baby's new life are a whirlwind of novelty and activity. People will be 'dropping in' at wildly inappropriate times to 'pay their respects' (see how rough the mother is looking, confirm the baby is yours, eat all your biscuits, proudly present you with battery-operated fluffy pink hippopotamuses that sing annoying songs when prodded or thrown against hard surface). This is strange and annoying and to be cherished, because you will rarely have this attention again as parents. Should you elect to breed again, don't expect anyone to turn up and see the second baby, let alone hand over expensive presents. You will do well to get the odd email. But a first baby always draws the crowds. One way to handle it is to arrange visits at a particular time each day, say between five and seven p.m. Then you can chuck them out before they start drinking all your wine and asking what time's dinner. (It also forestalls maternal exhaustion. Several new mothers I know said it felt like being in a zoo.) Do stock up on biscuits, though. No one will bring them. And you and your partner will also need a secret stash for yourself, for the hard times.

For there will be hard times. A newborn baby is more than a full-time job. It's about one and a half full-time jobs, with lots of unscheduled overtime. You will have to learn a great deal very quickly. Antenatal classes will have attempted to cover these early days with baby, but by that point in the course your brain was so full of contractions and epidurals there was no room for anything else. It was hard enough at that stage to imagine what the birth would be like; it was impossible to imagine what life would be like afterwards. So suddenly you are at home with your small baby, which cries half the time, wakes up at all hours of the day and the night and fills thousands of nappies in any 24-hour period. You learn fast because there's no choice. Some people say that newborn babies are anarchists. They are not. They are more like excessively demanding feudal warlords. Before the birth you probably lived your life with a fair degree of freedom. Within certain bounds you did much as you wanted to. Now you are an indentured servant, utterly at the mercy of a pint-sized tyrant who invariably issues orders with a furious cry. (The crying may not be that loud as yet. But as baby grows, so will its decibel output. In six months' time it will be like living with Concorde.)

And you may feel that you are not up to the task. If it's any consolation, this is the way everyone feels.

DUNCAN: I remember when we first brought J home, we had to give her a bath. We laid her down on the mat. Dinah and I were running in and out of the room, getting towels and stuff, and she was just lying there going 'Waaaah!' And we're saying to her, 'Look, we don't know what we're doing, either! This is new for us, too! Don't expect too much!'

IVAN: I continually felt I might not be up to the task. I still do, and I don't think that's anything unusual. You just do your best. And I think anybody who says they know how to bring up children is lying, or a fool. I still worry late at night, about my son, about my daughters, what I've said to them, what I've done, or whatever. It never goes away.

ANTHONY: Up to the task, no, never felt that at all. It was hard after R was born, because Astrid was so ill and knackered and down and we were a bit on our own. None of our family live locally and the parents are quite old. My mum's blind and got arthritis. Astrid's younger sister was quite cool, but my sister just disappeared off the map. So it was hard physically. I gave up work and did a lot of child care (R was on bottles from the first night) and didn't go anywhere. Oh, and it was Christmas and Astrid's sister and new husband stayed with us in Astrid's tiny flat. Um, busy. And it's never really eased off. You always want to do great, exciting, loving, supportive things, but somehow the washing-up comes first. I don't think I'm a bad dad at all, but it's such a slog.

The baby stares at you as though you are an idiot. And maybe you are. But the baby doesn't know that. All the baby is doing is growing. Everything is subsumed to this task. When your partner was pregnant, the baby's health and well-being always came first. That wasn't a conscious decision: the biology took care of it. Now baby is out in the world, you the father have joined the equation. Baby's needs still come first, but it's both you and your partner who will now be squeezed dry. At birth a typical baby weighs 7½lb. It will lose a couple of pounds in the first few days of life, as it adjusts to the sudden loss of its beloved placenta. A week later it will be back to birth weight and from then there is no looking back. Glug, glug, glug, glug. After five months Junior will have doubled its body weight, and will add the same again by its first birthday. Not even professional darts players can do this. At birth Junior is, on average, 20 inches tall (or long). A year later he or she will have added ten to twelve inches. His or her brain will have more than doubled its weight. The heart will be nearly twice the size. She could well be talking. He could well be walking.

Compared to most animals the human baby seems a vulnerable, rather weedy thing. A baby cow pops out, stands up, runs around a bit and that's it. End of childhood. Whereas our young are 18 or 19 before they finally leave home, go on terrible gap year holidays to the Far East and end up as drugs 'mules' for lipsmacking oriental villains. Human childhood lasts forever, primarily because of these large brains we have been saddled with. Chimps and apes reach sexual maturity far more quickly, and so did our distant hairy ancestors. But the great evolutionary tool that is our brain has developed beyond these modest origins, and now it needs all those years to acquire the knowledge to lead an independent life. (Until we move back home at 25, that is.)

In its first months a human baby seems virtually helpless. Note the use of the words 'seem' and 'virtually'. Babies may not do very much, but without the slightest effort they manage to get us, their parents, to run around doing everything on their behalf. In two decades' time we will be helping break them out of Thai or Vietnamese jails. The servitude never ends.

Vulnerable and weedy be damned. The human baby is an extraordinary creature, with extraordinary abilities. As well as growing, over the next year it will learn how to live. It is already amazingly alert, sensitive to its surroundings, watching, listening, soaking everything up. It is not staring at you because it thinks you are an idiot. It is trying to see what you are doing, who you are. It is acquiring knowledge. Everything is new. Everything is raw material. (All babies are writers. Discuss.)

Consider the amazing reflexes a baby is born with. The pre-smile is just one of many. Probably the most famous is the grasp reflex. Junior will grasp anything you put into its tiny hand. Play tug of war with your finger – and expect to lose. The more you pull your finger, the tighter it holds on. Already the little bleeder has the upper hand.

Some reflexes are easy to misinterpret. Stand your baby on a table and he/she will take an instinctive step forward. Does this mean Junior will walk early, have instinctive ball skills and one day play for England? Sadly not. It's just what they call the step reflex, and like most of these things it disappears after a few weeks. Put your baby stomach down on the table and, with luck, you'll witness the crawl reflex. Take your baby into the sea – on a warm day, ideally – and you will find it can swim, or at least, make reflex swimming movements to keep afloat. (An image memorably captured on the cover of Nirvana's *Nevermind* album.) If a baby believes it is falling, it may throw out its arms and legs in a star formation (this is called the Moro response). Most practical of all may be the rooting reflex. Stroke baby's cheek and it will automatically turn its head in that direction, looking for a nipple to suck. Fascinating to watch, although baby will start to get pissed off unless supplied with a real milk-engorged breast from time to time.

The abilities of the newborn continue to surprise the men in white coats who get research grants to look into this sort of thing. The Medical Research Council's Cognitive Development Unit have shown that babies recognise their mothers' faces from four days old. Again, they have no idea how this happens. A 1983 study found that some newborns could imitate an adult opening their mouth and sticking out their tongue – and they could do this when only half an hour old. (Imagine: you have just given birth, and some men in white coats rush in, pull faces at your baby, write down the results and rush out again. All in the name of knowledge.) This skill, if that's what it is, lapses after three weeks or so. Six months later the baby's ability to imitate returns as though it had never been away.

In *The Father's Book*, David Cohen gives a list of things to try with your baby in its first 24 hours of life. It's worth reproducing in full:

1. Make eye contact.
2. Look at your child and smile.
3. Tickle his or her toes.
4. Test the grasp reflex.
5. Stroke the baby gently.
6. Make ridiculous noises at the baby.
7. Watch for the baby imitating you.

If you don't find 'bonding' with your baby the most natural thing in the world – and many men don't – then treating it as an object of study may be more helpful than you know. But this sort of stimulation is what a baby is waiting for. Newborns process information as quickly as two-year-olds. Their brains are ready for everything life can throw at them, including strange men sticking tongues out at them.

Incidentally, not all of the baby's reflexes wear off after a few weeks. The survivors include the sneeze reflex (when nasal passages are irritated) and the yawn reflex (when additional oxygen is needed, or there's a boring documentary on TV). These and others will stay with baby for the rest of its life.

But as you begin to understand how much this immobile little lump can do, and its potential, you also begin to appreciate how fine a little baby's spirit is. They may cry a lot, but so would you if you had no other way of getting your needs met. The idea that babies are in some way malign or cunning – as previous generations often believed implicitly – is wrong, and has been wholly discredited. A baby needs you to look after it. Evolution has given it instincts and some reflexes and beautiful blue eyes to help it do this. The rest is up to you. It's not the baby who is the writer, it's the parent. The baby is the blank sheet of paper, and you are holding the pen. But we'll return to this later.

14 breasts

When white-bread teenager Debby Boone sang 'You Light Up My Life' in 1977, she was actually referring to God. If a heterosexual man sang it, he would almost certainly be addressing women's breasts. But the notion that such wondrous creations have a function as well as ornamental value, is one of the more startling facets of new fatherhood. In all our years thinking about breasts, I doubt many of us had concentrated too hard on the idea that breasts of our acquaintance would one day provide the only source of nourishment to a baby in which we had a well-documented 50 per cent genetic share. And yet the evidence is before us, often within minutes of birth. You've had one vast shock – a baby – and here's another.

Some fathers, I have to say, don't like it. Having formed an intimate alliance with the mother's breasts, they see their place taken by this greedy little latecomer who appears to have instant access to the precious globes. Indeed, over the next few months, your partner may only ever wear clothes that allow her to whip out a tit at a second's notice, in a way that you may have been trying to persuade her to do for some time. Junior has but a small stomach, and becomes hungry appallingly quickly. In public places he or she needs to be latched on in the fastest and most efficient way possible. Only a saint wouldn't feel jealous. Correction: only a dead female saint wouldn't feel jealous.

Nonetheless, breast milk is one of nature's little miracles, and it can help turn your other little miracle into a rather large miracle. For the first four months a breastfeeding baby will consume nothing else. Current advice has it that you should not introduce solids into the baby's diet until six months, although fashions change so fast in parenting that the autumn season's breastfeeding advice could be completely different. No one, though, argues about the value and general goodness of breast milk. It has everything the baby needs. In past generations everyone was told to bottle-feed, as formula milk was a scientific miracle created by huge unpleasant multinational companies unable to charge you for mammary use. It took 30 years or so, but the world finally saw through this. Formula milk was only ever an approximation of breast milk anyway. Why use the fake when the real thing is freely available?

This is not to say that breastfeeding is straightforward. It almost never is. Few mothers or babies take to it immediately and without a struggle. There is a technique to learn, which sounds easy enough when you are being told about it at antenatal classes, but can prove problematic when there's a real live baby to feed. If Junior doesn't clamp on right, if the mother is tense (and it's hard to see how she can be anything else), if a hundred small things don't quite work, the whole business can be hellish. Sore, cracked and even blistered nipples, blocked milk ducts, mastitis ... maybe we shouldn't be surprised that more than half of new mothers in the UK have given up on breastfeeding by six weeks.[11] Some are repelled by it, others overwhelmed by it; many just decide it's not for them. As always, respect her wishes. They are her breasts, after all.

Breastfeeding is fascinating to watch. Baby doesn't just suck at the breast, he or she clamps the whole mouth over it, creating a suction effect. (Unlike adults, babies can breathe and swallow at the same time.) And there isn't just one big hole, there are lots of little holes. Milk comes out of the nipple as water comes out of a sprinkler. It's common for one breast to produce far more milk than the other: even the smallest baby will soon work this out and start to declare a preference.[12]

Note that there is no connection between original breast size and milk production. I say 'original' because even the tiniest flea-bite breasts will attain milky grandeur by the time Junior homes in on them. They really are the most amazing piece of equipment. In each breast there are around 20 segments, or

---

11. Currently 69 per cent of mothers breastfeed at birth, 52 per cent two weeks later and 42 per cent at six weeks.

12. In our house the milkier breast was known fondly as Presumptuous Bosom. Both babies expressed a strong preference. Trying to cope with the flow made their eyes bulge.

lobes, each of which is made up of glands called alveoli which cluster together like bunches of grapes. Each alveolus is lined with milk-producing cells. During pregnancy, these previously dormant cells kick into action and the body also grows some new ones. When baby arrives and is shoved on the nipple, the sucking action stimulates the mother's pituitary gland, near the brain, which sends a hormone to the breast: this is the milk order, with a note for a couple of extra pints. The raw material for the milk is already in the bloodstream. I have seen it said that milk is essentially blood without the red blood cells, but that's a rather unappetising thought.

Although not as unappetising as the milk itself. Go on, have a slurp. Human milk is watery and sweet, less creamy than even the lowest fat cow's milk. (If your baby has a tooth, it will be a sweet one. Newborns actually have more taste buds than adults. As well as the ones on the tongue, the palate, the tonsils and the back of the throat, they also have a few on the insides of their cheeks. Our grown-up taste buds recognise five distinctive tastes; babies' identify only sweetness. Anything else tastes disgusting to them.)

Curiously, smaller breasts are better designed for feeding than the truly monumental. (I am assuming that the breasts are, indeed, a hundred per cent human breast and not augmented by artificial implants. Porn breasts may be good for male masturbatory purposes but they can be bloody useless as breasts.) Some mothers with substantial (real) breasts report that their baby is 'fighting at the breast'. They worry that the baby seems to be resisting the feed, whereas in truth the poor little bastard is struggling for air. If your mouth is full of nipple, and your nose is impeded by breast, breathing is always going to be a challenge. All breasts are a combination of fatty tissue and glandular tissue. It's the glandular tissue that feeds babies, and the fatty tissue that tends to enrapture their fathers. If there was only glandular tissue, women would be flat-chested when they weren't suckling their babies – rather like chimps and monkeys. Yet another reason, in case you needed one, not to be a chimp or a monkey.

Still, both chimps and monkeys know that the best time to feed your babies is when they are hungry. Until relatively recently this is not what mothers did. For many years, convention had it that babies should only be fed at precise intervals. Some experts said every hour and a half. Other experts said two hours. A third group of experts, anxious to show their independence from the first two groups of experts, insisted on two and a half hours. After a few weeks, mother and baby would settle into a routine of four-hourly feeds. There was only one problem with this. Baby couldn't tell the time.

So when it was hungry, baby would cry. Mother, instructed not to feed baby until 2.45 whatever happened, would have to listen to these desperate wails until the clock clicked 2.45 and the baby got its stomach-full. The theory was that baby had to 'get used' to the mother's regimen, as though it had previously been plotting and planning to overthrow the household like a tiny communist agitator. The result was that baby was made miserable and insecure, and when it finally did get to feed it wouldn't stop feeding, because it knew it wouldn't be getting the milk it would need the next time it was hungry. To this day some experts continue to insist on rigidly timetabled feeds, as part of a programme of rigid timetables. This is a Third Reich view of childcare, concerned only with implementing order. Nurture isn't on the radar. According to one NCT tutor, such experts don't understand that 'breastfeeding is a relationship between a mother and her baby, not just a way to get milk into it.'

The breastfeeding 'debate' – I'm not sure it's ever quite as civilised as that – is a perfect example of the way parents are bombarded with advice, much of it cancelling each other out, and are then made to feel guilty when things don't work out for them. Of the half of British mothers who give up breast-feeding within six weeks, 90 per cent are said to regret it later. This is the worst of both worlds. Baby doesn't get the goodness of breast milk, and mother beats herself up about it afterwards. By the same token there are experts telling you to demand-feed, other experts telling you to feed to a timetable ... Everyone knows they are right – except the poor bloody parents, who end up thinking they are wrong about every-thing. The fact is that bottle feeding is never going to do anyone any harm. Bottle-fed babies are not going to get fewer 'A' levels or fail to win Olympic gold medals (well, not because they were bottle-fed, anyway). Breast may be best, but bottle is fine. The main disadvantage, of course, is that your workload will be drastically increased by bottle-feeding. Because you no longer have an excuse not to, you will now be the one getting up in the middle of the night to answer the infant's cries. The main advantage is that once milk production has ceased –

which happens of its own accord – your access to said breasts will no longer be denied.

Of course, some men actually enjoy bottle-feeding.

> *ANTHONY: Astrid didn't find it easy feeding R, and she was back at work after three months so I did quite a lot of bottle feeds with him. We were lucky he swapped between the two at will; so I did a lot of feeds myself, especially when Astrid was back at work. I enjoyed it. Very peaceable. But I was jealous I couldn't breastfeed – honest. Did I mention the exploding breasts? I just think it's the most amazing reflex that lactating mums start to lactate as soon as they hear a crying baby. So Astrid's breasts were going off all over the place, even when I was feeding R. Our second one has been breastfed throughout, so I've barely been involved. But now we're in the middle of weaning and trying to get him to take a bottle from me. He's slowly coming round. When he's desperate I'm sure he will.*

Many parents go for a mixture of breast and bottle, depending on circumstance. There's the issue of breastfeeding in public – and to many people it is, still, an issue. Countless times I have been with my girlfriend in public places when she has flopped out a milk-heavy breast for a small child seeking dairy fulfilment. And countless times people have turned and stared. They are often older, with pinched mouths (if women) or pinched beards (if men). 'There is a time and a place for that,' they appear to be thinking, and may even say out loud. That time is not now and that place is not here. But baby is hungry now and here. Many mothers are intimidated by people's disapproval. Some use bottles to avoid potential embarrassment. I can understand that; what I don't get is why anyone else should disapprove. Who are they to judge? And would they seriously prefer the child to scream its head off, just so they can be protected from the briefest flash of womanly flesh? In this century?[13]

Breastfeeding does change breasts. Firmness is the first casualty. A well nibbled breast will be more pendulous than it might once have been. If I had eaten a biscuit every time a mother has told me that her breasts now 'hang down to her knees', I would now weigh 19 stone. They don't, of course. It's just what they say to taunt and terrify you. After all, unless your breast experience is wide, you may never have encountered post-feeding breasts before. You certainly don't see them in popular culture. Tilda Swinton is the only actress I can think of who has appeared in a film with bare breasts that have obviously seen baby action. (I saw them in the 2003 film *Young Adam*. You may well have spotted them elsewhere.) And there's nothing wrong with Tilda's. Cosmetic surgeons like to imply that breasts are in some way deformed by breastfeeding and should therefore be renewed by expensive surgery. These people prey on the vulnerable and unconfident and must be resisted, at least until the law is changed to allow us to murder them in cold blood.

---

13. The US, of course, is even more rampantly breast-phobic. When the singer Janet Jackson inadvertently flashed her right breast on TV in February 2004, one Terri Carlin, a bankworker from Tennessee, issued a writ against the broadcasting corporations she held responsible. 'As a direct and proximate result of the broadcast,' the writ proclaimed, viewers of the breast 'were caused to suffer outrage, anger, embarrassment and serious injury.' Everybody around the world wondered the same thing. Serious injury? Ms Carlin dropped the case three days later.

15

piss, shit and vomit

BASIL: Words that summarise the first year in its entirety. I soon learned that if I threw out every item of my clothing that had been peed, shat or puked on I would be stark-bollock naked within two months. It was only in my first year of fatherhood that I truly understood what my sister-in-law meant by a 'poo-tastrophe'.

You don't need me to tell you that babies piss, shit and vomit pretty much all of the time. Food enters via the mouth, but leaves by a variety of routes, none of them predictable. Some babies helpfully look ill just before they chuck up. Others seem to be smiling, and one or two might even chuckle. Again, this may be in your imagination, but one thing is for certain: in 30 seconds' time milky sick will be all over the place. At the same moment, the infant bladder being tiny and hyperactive, the baby is almost certainly doing a pee, and may have a shit saved up, too. That nappy could be filling up faster than a Tokyo train in the rush hour. What to do? Where to start? Which cloth to use? What's on TV?

PISS

Funnily enough, this is not the worst of your problems. The extraordinary sponge-like qualities of modern-day nappies – you could pour most of a reservoir into one without unduly discomforting the wearer – mean that you don't actually have to change them every time baby does a pee. Indeed, you can often wait until the nappy is about the same weight as the baby itself. (If the baby is walking, this usefully develops the thigh muscles, although the noise of the piss-saturated nappy swishing along the ground may disturb passers-by.) The big question, of course, is whether to go for disposables, and thus doom the planet, or selflessly use 'terry' nappies, and thus doom yourself and your partner to endless domestic drudgery. For the ecologically-minded and rich who live in big cities, there are services that turn up every day to take away dirty 'terry' nappies and bring back nice clean ones. I know people who have looked into this and talked about it very enthusiastically, before buying disposables like everybody else. And if our great-great-great-great-grandchildren end up having to build their cities on vast mounds of undecayed twenty-first-century Huggies, that's just tough.[14]

In early infancy, then, piss is a breeze – it doesn't even smell of anything much when you do come into contact with it. You are more likely to come into contact with it if you have a small boy, whose pee generally travels in a pleasing parabolic arc

14. That said, the statistics are a little scary. Eight million disposable nappies head for landfill sites in the UK *every day*. They take between 200 and 500 years to decompose. In a household with one baby, disposable nappies make up half of all household rubbish.

defined in Cartesian terms by the equation $y^2=4ax$. With a newborn boy the most dangerous moment is when you take off his nappy. The sudden change of temperature activates the bladder, and if you are not ready with a muslin or something to staunch the flow, you will be changing your shirt in three or four minutes' time. Splashes in the eye are not uncommon. One mother I know got a squirt right up her nose.

It's when your baby hits the age of two, and starts potty-training, that urine will really make an impact on your life. On your life, on your carpet, on most pieces of furniture, and on your trousers if the baby is sitting on your lap at the time. Baby wants to pee in the potty. Really wants to. But baby keeps forgetting to ask. And you keep forgetting to ask baby. Then, during the commercial break, the tell-tale trickle down the tiny trousers, necessitating a complete change of clothes and a sizeable wodge of kitchen roll to mop up the excess. It's even worse when it happens out of doors. Then the phrase 'piss is a breeze' assumes a whole new meaning.

SHIT

Babies are astoundingly effective crapping machines. Our adult bowels have been wrecked by stress and thousands of bacon butties, but newborns process their mother's milk with impressive speed, and can expel the residue anything up to three or four times a day.[15] This is the part of the job most dreaded by

15. It takes breast milk an average of 15 hours to pass through the digestive system, and formula milk about twice as long.

new fathers. Being male we are naturally more squeamish than females. Our pain threshold is much lower, our physical cowardice more pronounced, and our desire to clean up a baby's shit pretty much non-existent. Of all fathers I spoke to, 89 per cent agreed with the statement 'Changing nappies was the thing I most feared before I became a father.' (This 89 per cent also thought that the other eleven per cent were lying.) New fathers anxious to impress friends and family, not to mention social workers, will take any opportunity to change a nappy in public to show that they can do it without (a) throwing up or (b) spilling baby cack all over the floor. It could be the most visible rite of passage that new fatherhood offers. It is also, to be frank, a piece of cake. Changing nappies is so much less appalling than you think it's going to be that, in a strange sort of way, you almost end up enjoying it. Were it not for the enormous quantities of excrement involved, you could nearly call it a hobby.

Nature helps in this. There are several discrete phases in the development of baby's shit which ease the terrified father into his new routine. And because it's your own baby, and you are quite well disposed towards it, you won't mind at all. WARNING: Changing other people's children's nappies is a wholly disgusting experience and should be avoided at all costs.

PHASE 1: MECONIUM

This is the baby's first shit, and a striking substance it is. Jet black, with an unearthly green tinge, and as sticky as high-tensile industrial adhesive, meconium is essentially the packing for the digestive system that hasn't been used yet. Fortunately it doesn't smell. This is true. You dare not breathe in, in case it's the last time you ever do – but it is genuinely odour-free. Just make sure you don't get it on your clothes. For as placenta is supposed to be delicious if lightly grilled and served with horseradish and a full bodied red wine, so meconium makes an excellent rudimentary asphalt. If you have a driveway that needs doing, and twins, you could be in luck.

PHASE 2: BUTTERY

Meconium smells of nothing, and the cack generated by breast milk smells strangely of butter. Imagine your child's digestive system as a huge churn, with slightly salted Anchor Spreadable the natural result. And my word, is it spreadable. Before solids enter your child's diet, excrement is a dangerous and slippery substance that can fill a nappy in seconds. Modern nappy technology is advanced, but even the most tightly fitted Pamper won't keep the full squirt in all of the time. If it doesn't go down one leg, it'll go down the other. And when the baby sits down, any left over will shoot straight up its back. This will calm down later, I promise, but for the moment you can expect two or three complete changes of clothes per baby per day. Many babies' clothes spend more time being washed than being worn. It is just as well that the cack smells buttery, for if it didn't, you'd probably kill yourself. The extraordinary thing is, you get used to it quite quickly. Honest. Trust me on this. After you have changed

20 or 30 nappies, you will do it so automatically you will barely notice you are doing it at all.

(This is how to spot fathers who never change nappies. They always tell you how much they hate changing nappies.)

In fact – and here's the greatest shock – you may actually find you quite like the smell of your baby's shit. After all, it is buttery.

It's when this has happened that you realise that you really have become one of those Sad New Dads, who will be boring all his friends with how rewarding fatherhood is, and thus eventually alienating everyone in the whole world.

Formula milk is said to produce nastier shit than breast milk. Apparently it's green in tinge and clears your sinuses like a Fisherman's Friend. But I haven't knowingly smelled it myself, so cannot confirm this.

PHASE 3: SOLIDS

After four months or so, baby will start eating solid foods and its excrement will change. Less buttery, more foody. More solid. More shitty, in truth. And it will change colour each day, depending on what Junior has been eating. Lots of carrots = orange poo. If baby starts eating meat, the shit becomes as foul and revolting as any adult's. Worse, in some ways, because adult shit rarely gets under your fingernails.

But Mother Nature is a cunning old bird. By the time baby is ingesting solids, you should be so used to changing nappies that you can take the vile odours in your stride. If we had to deal with them at birth, no one would ever change a nappy. Some men don't. Having avoided changing one when the shit smelled of nothing, they find it impossible to make the great leap when it starts smelling of Whiskas Supermeat. The learning curve is gentle in the early weeks, but by six to eight months it is the north face of the Eiger. And by then a man who cannot change a nappy is a pitiful figure, liable to be held in contempt by all humanity. When a well-known media chef revealed on television that he had never changed a nappy, the audience hissed. He thought he had done something clever; they thought he was a wuss. He was astounded. He thought all the men, at least, would admire and respect his stance. But he had spent too much time in restaurant kitchens terrorising minions. Without him realising it, the parameters of machismo had changed. These days, Real Men Wipe Arses.

When you start wiping, you do so with forensic care and a huge amount of kit. Midwives, health visitors and other well-informed busybodies will advise that you need the following: a couple of clean nappies; some cotton wool (to clean off the poo); a bowl of warm water (to rinse cotton wool in); a towel (to dry baby's precious arse); a box of wet wipes (to clean it again, this time properly); some talcum powder (to powder precious arse); some zinc barrier cream (to protect arse from nappy rash); kitchen roll (to mop up the terrible mess you have just made); foul-perfumed nappy bags (to put dirty nappy in); three toys and four cloth books to distract baby with; large drink for Daddy to calm nerves. All of which takes so long that baby has probably done another load, so you have to start again straight away.

Two weeks later most of this stuff is in the bathroom somewhere and forgotten. All you really need are the nappies, the wet wipes, a couple of bits of kitchen roll for emergencies and the vital barrier cream. For parents of small babies Sudocrem will become as familiar a word as lunch, dinner or divorce. It's marvellous stuff. It protects against nappy rash, and because it is antiseptic, it cures nappy rash if you forgot to put it on last time. And by now you will be able to change a nappy, even one with crap dripping out of it, in two minutes or less. While talking on the phone and drinking a cup of tea. It couldn't be easier.

(Soon you will even be able to tell when your baby is pushing one out. The early buttery poos make wonderful deafening farty noises, but seem to require little effort on the part of baby. But once the solids kick in, baby begins to strain and stretch, grunting slightly as its eyes cross and bulge with the effort of it all. When it's all over, a look of sublime satisfaction crosses baby's face. If you ever see anything funnier in your life you will be very lucky.)

VOMIT

Piss is nothing. Shit can be managed. But vomit defeats the best of us. I was lucky: neither of my two threw up much. Some little ones barf by the hour. It's random and uncontrollable, and for a couple of months you too will walk around the house with a muslin constantly draped over one shoulder, just in case.

The baby's stomach, like most of its internal organs, is not yet operating at full throttle. Unlike new cars, babies do not come already run in. They will ingest the customary titful of milk and then bring a certain percentage back up, often on the parental shoulder as you wind them. These vomblobs are known in the trade as 'possets'. Muslins guard against possets. You are speaking a different language these days, one that has only tangential contact with English as you knew it before. Also you smell of sick a lot of the time. However careful you are, small blobs find their way onto every item of clothing you own. After a while you don't even notice. Unfortunately everybody else does. Non-parents shake their heads with pity, and learn to hold their breath like synchronised swimmers. There is nothing you can do about any of this.

And it could be worse. You could have a projectile vomiter. My friend Georgia had one of these. He only P.V.ed ten or 15 times in three months, but each occasion would have won Oscars for special effects and cinematography. There was never any warning. Her son had glugged at the breast as usual. Then suddenly, a Linda Blair-like spray of milky spew would shoot out of his mouth. A fireman's hose couldn't have done a better job. If anyone had been sitting ten feet away, they would have been drenched. Georgia stopped going out. It was too dangerous. She never knew when he might strike. Restaurants were an impossibility. It would have been like dining with her own miniature Mr Creosote. Even going to the shops to buy a pint of milk was fraught with peril. This was in the depths of winter, so she would wrap him up in half a dozen layers, wrap herself up in half a dozen layers, strap him in the sling, put the sling on, get to the door, feel the fireman's hose of vomit hit her chest, stand still for a moment, scream, bang her head against the wall a couple of times, go back inside, take all his and her clothes off and wash them both and shove everything in the washing machine, put more clothes on and start the whole process all over again. By the time she reached the shop she had forgotten why she was going there.

Projectile vomiters have their uses. As pure spectacle they are remarkable. If by some fluke you can get them to do it to order, you could sell them to a circus. Or go to a party and aim your vomiter at someone you don't like. Or put on some roller skates, strap your vomiter to your back facing away from you, and use him or her as a jet pack. Projectile vomiting is an infant reflex, and like the others it is gone after three months. You might as well make the most of it while you can.

16 waaaaaaaaaaaaaaaah!

Babies cry. There's no escaping it. Crying is their way of telling you that something is wrong. Desmond Morris in *Babywatching* lists seven main causes of crying: Pain, Discomfort, Hunger, Loneliness, Over-stimulation, Under-stimulation and Frustration. That's life for small babies. Their needs are few, but they are fundamental. Babies themselves cannot satisfy these needs. They cannot move, feed themselves, cover or uncover themselves, change their own nappies, open a window or turn off the CD player. So when they need something done they open their lungs and bawl for Britain. See that epiglottis wobble. Hear that noise in the next postal district. Run round the room like a headless chicken wondering what to do next.

Many mothers, who in previous centuries would have been

identified as witches and burnt at the stake, claim to be able to tell the difference between all the various cries. Good for them. Sadly, no father I have ever heard of can do this. One or two claim they can, but they are the sort of men who do claim things. There is no need to listen too closely to anything they say. Witchy mothers, then, can sort out their infant's problem within a few seconds, and go back to their cauldron. The rest of us panic and swear. Crying can erode the parental sanity; it can fracture relationships; it can turn neighbours into lifelong enemies, if your walls are thin enough. And that's the idea. Baby needs your attention. Crying that people notice is doing its job.

Morris's list is useful if incomplete. First, Pain. Babies may have internal pains as a result of the birth process; later on they may have colic or be teething (more of both shortly); later yet, when they start to move, they will start to bump and bash themselves. The pain cry is raw, and may even be aggrieved. Even to a tiny baby, pain can seem magnificently unjust. 'Why me?' the cry says. This is only the first of your child's questions that you won't be able to answer.

Discomfort usually means you have not changed the nappy since the last full moon. Look out for clues, such as a blinding smell of excrement, or nappy rash like second-degree burns. Maybe baby has a little indigestion. Did a breastfeeding mama eat curry last night? Everything goes into the breast milk, and from there into baby (a large glass of red wine often does wonders for a tired and gloomy mother, and for breastfeeding baby two or three hours later).

Hunger is straightforward. Give baby breast or bottle and all the world's problems are solved. To a small baby happiness is a warm nipple. 43 years later I feel the same about pizza: the programming hasn't failed me yet.

Loneliness is an interesting one. Are you reading the paper in the other room when you should be looking after baby? Of course you are. Babies start to feel insecure if left alone too long. They are social animals, who thrive on love and attention. Beware, too, of Over-stimulation. This can mean many things: too many people in the room, music too loud, too many sharp and bright images on TV. Babies cannot process sensory information as adults can. (Some experts believe you should not let a child watch TV at all before the age of six months, and only sparingly before two years.)

Under-stimulation and Frustration afflict slightly older babies. After six months or so babies can become bored with terrifying ease, until given a cardboard box to sit in. (Or you can turn on the TV.) Then they will cry with frustration as their desire to do something outstrips their ability to do it. It's tough being a baby. Curiously Morris does not mention Tiredness, which I would have thought was every bit as important as the others. Very young babies go to sleep at will, but as they spend more of their days awake, they find it harder and harder to drop off. Sometimes a baby moves beyond sleep, into a region familiar to anyone who has found themselves watching Steven Seagal films on TV at 2.30 in the morning. A tired cry can be a pitiful thing to hear, so switch off the television this minute, and go to bed.

So what are you supposed to do with this crying baby? The standard male response is to feign death and hope that someone else in the house will deal with it. One father I know looks for a woman, any woman, to sort out the problem, and that includes neighbours and passers-by. But suppose you are not in a position to delegate. Suppose it is you in the house alone, with a crying baby in the next room and an unread newspaper burning your fingertips. Is it the act of a responsible adult to hide your head under the cushion and/or turn the TV up to full volume?

Clearly not. So you go into the baby and pick it up, reasoning that it is better to do something than to do nothing, especially if you are to be called to account for your actions later on. In fact this is sound thinking. Even if you haven't the faintest idea what to do next, picking it up tells baby that you are there and you care. Baby does not know that the only thing you care about is baby shutting up. Baby does not need to know. Baby recognises the love and affection you have to offer, and with a bit of luck, responds to it. Babies need cuddling as fiercely as they need food or sleep. Rocking and swaying and kissing and nuzzling might just do the trick.

A word here on general policy. It's important when a baby cries not to convince yourself that he or she is trying to 'manipulate' you or get one up on you. You don't have to be even slightly paranoid to reach this conclusion; all you need is to be tired and anxious, which describes all of us at one time or other. Later on, as baby turns into toddler and starts to learn the rules of life, it might well try to get its own way by any means possible. Tiny babies, though, are as capable of manipulating you as they are of playing snooker. Their needs are primal. *They cannot survive without you.* If you can rid yourself of all thoughts of manipulation, and just accept that for a while you are this baby's slave, you will be more relaxed and so better placed to solve baby's problems. Whereas if you believe baby is wrapping you around its little finger, you will be too busy thinking about this to solve baby's problems, which could make things worse.

Everyone has an opinion on this. Respond quickly to your baby's cries and clucking old busybody relatives will be sure to tell you that you are teaching the child 'bad habits'. They may even use the S-word. 'You spoil that child, you do.' Send these ancients on their way. If you want to teach a baby 'bad habits' the best way is to ignore it completely. Then it becomes clingy and attention-seeking or worse: it withdraws into itself, expecting nothing from anybody. Boys, for some reason, get more of this 'tough love', which does no one any good.

As it happens, it is literally impossible to spoil a baby. All but the most brutal childcare experts agree on this. Oh yes, you can buy too many toys for your baby, feed it *foie gras* and take it on holidays to the Bahamas, but none of this will make the smallest impact (other than the *foie gras,* which will give it the most appalling bellyache). Love and affection are what babies need, and virtually all they need, beyond the basics. You can never cuddle a baby too much. And all this matters most in the first weeks of its life. This is when the template is set, when the ways baby will respond to you and to the rest of humanity are to a great extent defined.

In the long run, then, it's not the crying that matters, it's how you react to the crying. The fact is, some babies will cry more than others. The circumstances of the birth might have a bearing on it. If the mother had a general anaesthetic, if baby was eased out with the mighty forceps, if baby had to endure a long labour – all these are believed to make babies cry more later on. Also, newborn boys often cry more than newborn girls. No one knows why: it just is.

Which means, slightly terrifyingly, that there may not be a problem you can solve at all. You may simply have a baby that cries. These are not rational beings we are dealing with. They are not predictable. Baby cries. Pick up baby. Baby stops crying. Put baby down again. Baby starts crying again. Then, next time: baby cries. Pick up baby. Baby goes on crying. Put down baby. Baby stops crying. Partner picks up baby. Baby cries. Partner hands baby to you. Baby stops crying. Partner goes into sulk. And so on and so on. Every possible permutation of events is happening right now to some poor bastard of a parent within ten miles of where you are sitting.

Men, of course, tend to see life as a series of problems to be solved. And if a problem can't be solved? Even psychologists have noticed that fathers often deal less than brilliantly with a baby's emotional turmoil. 'A young father said, "I feed him, change him, play rough and tumble, I can't take any more." The mother was more in touch with the baby and could hold him and accept his distress. Father had to act to make it better and couldn't tolerate the distress.'[16] What makes it worse is that, somehow, you feel that you are the only person who has ever

16. From Judith Trowell's introduction to *The Importance of Fathers: A Psychoanalytic Re-Evaluation.*

had to endure this. You are not. Babies have cried for tens of thousands of years, and if anyone knew of a sure-fire cure, we might have heard about it by now. Indeed, around the world and throughout history, grown-ups have tried to put a different spin on crying babies, presumably to relieve their own suffering. In Japan every spring they hold crying baby competitions, for they believe that the more a baby cries, the stronger and healthier it will be as an adult. In Christian tradition, if a baby cried at its baptism, that was a sign to everyone that the Devil was being driven away. And not at all a sign that the baby did not like being dunked head first in a fontful of greasy cold water.

One possible explanation for non-stop crying is colic. Or, as some of the books call it, 'colic' (just as morning sickness is now 'morning' sickness). Many babies between the ages of three weeks and four months cry for no apparent reason. It usually strikes towards the end of the parenting day, when you are at your tiredest and most bad-tempered, but can crop up at other times of the day as well. It can last anything up to three or even four hours. It's called colic, a wonderfully old-fashioned name I always think, because colicky babies tend to pull their legs up and arch their backs as though they have severe stomach aches. Many experts call it 'colic' with the inverted commas because no one knows what causes it, although they don't think it's stomach ache. (A few experts won't even call it 'colic'. They call it 'what people understand by the term "colic"'. Any expert this detached from the parenting process can be safely ignored.)

Unfortunately you and I and everyone else who encounters

colic must work on the assumption that it is a stomach ache because that is what it looks like and seems like. You would guess, as you watch your small person doubling up in pain, that he or she has eaten something appalling – a 20p piece, for instance, or the decayed remains of a small rodent. But Junior is still on breast or bottle at this stage, so that can't be it. (It will be in a few months' time, when your baby starts experimenting with different foodstuffs – or 'foodstuffs', as the experts would probably call them.) There is simply no explanation for colic, and almost nothing you can do to relieve it. (Try laying your baby face down across your knees, support its little bawling head and gently massage its back. It might work, it might not.)

Colic can drive you barmy. As the days stretch out to weeks and even months, you keep on wondering, what the bloody hell is wrong in there? You will never know. One day the colic will simply stop. A week later you will have forgotten your baby ever had it. Remarkably, colic seems to have no long-term effects on your baby's well-being or general good cheer. Indeed, soon after its disappearance is when many parents record their baby's first smile. It may be that colic is a rite of passage certain babies have to undergo. Their parents accompany them through it, endure it with them, celebrate when it's all over. As long as they haven't topped themselves in the meantime.

At least colic comes to an end. Teething, as one baby expert put it, 'starts at six months and goes on until the age of 20.' Unless your baby is one of those authoritarian political leaders born with a rogue tooth, you probably won't even have thought about dentition (another glorious technical term) until it happens. Nonetheless, those teeth have been waiting under the gum since the womb, ready to strike. Their emergence provides a new and unexpected source of pain for baby, who will start frantically chewing on things to ease the discomfort. Teething babies also dribble a lot. They get bright red cheeks and can double as Belisha beacons. And they cry and cry and cry. You can put teething gel on their gums, give them something to chew other than your partner's nipple and wait for it to end. And then wait for it to begin again. Unlike colic, though, teething has an end-product: teeth. You may miss the gummy look, and coo over old photographs of your little toothless one, but the teeth represent real, measurable progress. For instance, you can measure the indentation on your finger when baby bites you. Now it's someone else's turn to cry.

So how to soothe your crying baby? There are several well-tested methods. Billions of people have been testing them over thousands of years. Occasionally one of them works.

- **The supine position.** Lie down on your back and lay your baby on your chest. They like the sound of the heartbeat, apparently. Rub your baby's back. Go to sleep. Snore like gurgling drain.

- **The tour of the house.** Hold baby upright and lean him/her against your shoulder. (Make sure you have put a muslin there first to protect your clothes from dribble and rogue possets.) Wander around your home singing old pop songs badly. Blush when caught by partner.

● **Use a sling.** For a tiny baby, get one that is made only of cloth. (The ones with aluminium exoskeletons are for babies of six months and older.) Strap in Junior and you can walk around, do the washing up, go to the pub, have sex with strangers in the park ... anything, really, as long as you keep moving, because that will loll Junior off to sleep. Babies love slings. Again, it's the contact, the beating heart, and Daddy's clothes smelling of sweat and drink.

● **Grandparents.** Remember, grandparents are not just for Christmas, they are for the whole year round. Unfortunately, many young people are so desperate to get away from their parents that when they come to have children themselves they find they have moved 400 miles or more from free babysitting. This is a waste of a valuable resource. Few grandparents have anything much to do, and quite a few have enough money to enable them not to do it. So they might as well be taking your baby off your hands for a few hours, and perhaps 'lending' you a tenner so you can go to the cinema. If they start droning on about your spoiling the baby or teaching it bad habits, threaten to put them in a home. (Your parents will always be much better with your children than they were with you. They will give them millions of treats, the same treats in fact that they used to deny you, just as your grandparents gave you the same treats they denied your parents. *This pattern can never be broken.*)

● **Dummy.** The 'D' word. Vast hairy stigmas have attached themselves to this harmless implement. Just as people who know nothing about language are vaguely aware that a split infinitive is A Bad Thing, so everyone knows that dummies are the tool of the devil. Serial killers Jeffrey Dahmer and Dr Harold Shipman both sucked dummies well into their teenage years.[17] Possibly because we have all seen them being shoved into toddlers' mouths by fishwives in supermarkets, we may associate dummies with a more primitive level of parenthood than that to which we aspire. It's pure snobbery. Most childcare experts cannot bring themselves to recommend their use without a string of caveats (such as 'Don't use them at all'). But dummies – or pacifiers as Americans call them, with their matchless gift for euphemism – have been around for centuries. You can see fifteenth-century dummies in the Ashmolean Museum at Oxford. Only around a third of babies find a use for dummies, and it may only be a brief phase before baby finds and starts sucking its thumb. For some babies, though, dummies do the trick, and that has to be better than endless crying. The main thing is not to sweeten the dummy with fruit juice or honey (unless you don't mind having fat children with no teeth). Also, according to many books, you should sterilise the dummy before every use. Oh yes, you're definitely going to do that.[18]

---

17. I have just made this up, but try telling a few people and see if they believe it.
18. There's an awful load of old bollocks talked about sterilisation. Although many parents become frantic about it, there's no evidence that non-stop sterilisation makes your baby any safer or healthier. Look at hospitals, which are supposed to pay closer attention to the killing of germs than most environments. Not only do they find it impossible to be completely sterile, but their attempts to do so have contributed to the growth of so-called 'superbugs', which are immune to everything. As a rule, cleanliness is more important than sterilising. A normal, everyday level of cleanliness is all you need to keep your family safe.

- **The cranial osteopath.** This is not something your GP would necessarily recommend, especially if he or she is the type who would rather put you on a course of antibiotics than work out what's wrong with you. But cranial osteopathy helped our youngest with his colic, and may do the job for you. The bones of the skull are not completely fused, even in adults. A cranial osteopath, by placing hands on the patient's head, claims to be able to feel minute rhythmic pulsations of the cranial bones and membranes. And if you remember how compressed a baby's skull is during birth, it makes sense that a little rudimentary correction of the head bones could improve matters. As one practitioner has put it, 'The natural tendency of the body is to heal itself. The cranial osteopath facilitates this process by helping to balance tissue tensions between his hands. The body then makes its own correction to a more tuned state.'[19] I have watched one in action: they barely seem to do anything, and you begin to wonder whether you haven't been ripped off by the new age equivalent of a fairground charlatan. But babies love it. Cranial osteopathy did not cure our boy of his colic; it eased it. At the time, though, that was more than enough.

If nothing else works, cuddle. Most babies love being cuddled. They can be so full of food they look as though they will burst. They can be amused and entertained to the point of coma. They can gurgle at brightly coloured pieces of plastic attached to their cot for only so long. But they can't be cuddled enough. They

---

19. Nicholas Handoll, quoted in *The Independent*.

crave physical affection. Some fathers find it hard to give, maybe because they weren't given enough themselves when they were babies. That was the wisdom then; we know better now. Even if it is colic and the baby won't stop crying for three months, you will glean the benefit of all that cuddling when the colic does subside. One day the baby will look up at you and smile, and everything will be as it should be. And the baby will never know that on 63 separate occasions you wanted to throw it out of the window. (Unless you did throw it out of the window.) If you can learn to comfort your baby as well as your partner can – which usually only takes perseverance and the will to do it – you will be amazed by how satisfying it is. Some fathers discover, to their vain delight, that they are better at comforting their child than their partners. It helps to be as relaxed as possible as you rock them out of their misery and, with luck, into a long deep sleep. I find that half a bottle of red wine helps, but each to his own.

17
sleep

'The horror of getting up is unparalleled, and I am filled with amazement every morning when I find that I have done it.' LYTTON STRACHEY

A newborn baby knows no night, knows no day. For a while you will be in the same terrible state of flux. It's like infinite jetlag. New parents talk of little else. Newish parents start talking about something else, then give up and go back to sleep deprivation. They are too tired to think. Their feet drag, their shoulders slump. Their eyes are like pissholes in the snow. Their babies, needless to say, are full of life and energy. The babies are getting the sleep they need. It's the parents who are losing their minds, their youth, their grip on reality. You think you look rough now? Look again in a year's time. Your closest relatives won't know it's you – and not because you'll have had plastic surgery and fled the country to avoid your responsibilities. The shitty nappies may not get to you; the lack of sleep will.

I am writing this on a Wednesday morning. The last four nights I have had five hours, six hours, four and a half hours and five and a half hours' sleep respectively. My daughter is four and a half, and my son will soon be two. We should be past the worst of it by now. But we aren't. Sadly I had a bit to drink last night. I am therefore a little hungover and rather bad-tempered. In the mirror this morning I looked older than my late grandfather. After lunch I shall go to the local public library, where there's an unusually comfortable armchair ...

This chapter will be split into handy gobbet-sized chunks for the convenience of sleep-deprived parents who may not be able to digest more than a single paragraph at a time.

THEY SLEEP AND THEY SLEEP AND THEY SLEEP

It's true – newborn babies sleep an awful lot. On average, according to Desmond Morris, they snooze for 16 hours and 36 minutes every day. This figure starts to fall almost immediately, but even five-year-olds should put in twelve solid hours. And yet newborn baby sleep is a fragile thing. Between half and two-thirds of it is light sleep, from which they can wake depressingly easily. Even the way they go to sleep is different. As overworked adults, we can hit the pillow, pass out and be snoring like warthogs within eight to ten seconds. Babies, by contrast, start with 20 minutes or so of light sleep before descending into big fat sleep, and it is only then that they truly settle. You may have to rock your little one and/or sing rude songs to ease the passage into deep sleep. Only when their eyes have stopped twitching is it safe to leave the room. Then you step on the creaky floorboard outside, and the whole process begins again.

NIGHT AND DAY

For the first six to ten weeks, baby cannot tell the difference. When tired, baby sleeps. When not tired, baby sits around gurgling or roars its lungs out. The fact that it's 3.30 in the morning and you have only been asleep since 1.15 makes no difference. And as soon becomes clear, there is no point trying to get a baby to sleep when it is full of beans. King Canute would have had more chance with the waves.

The single identifiable advantage of all this is that baby will drop off under what to us would be entirely hostile conditions. Light, dark, in bright sunshine, under floodlights – it makes no difference if baby is tired. They are far more sensitive to variations in temperature. They really are unutterably strange.

NOISE

Again, less of a problem than you would think. Baby likes to hear all the usual household noises – people clumping up and down the stairs, eating snack foods, calling each other bastards. There is no need to tiptoe around as infant is falling asleep. Indeed, it might actually be counter-productive, as by doing this you can unwittingly train your baby to need complete silence at bedtime. Fine if you are moving to the Outer Hebrides; otherwise a catastrophe in the making, especially now that Guy Fawkes Night is celebrated in most British towns and cities every night between 31 August and 5 January.

SMELL

According to one book I read, you should avoid going into your newborn baby's room too often to check whether it is still alive, as your smell could wake it. Well, there's something else to worry about. Am I a bad parent, or is it just my feet?

QUIZ TIME

If a baby wakes every two to six hours to be fed during the first six months of life, is that

(i) Unspeakable?
(ii) Unreasonable?
(iii) Perfectly normal?
(iv) Someone else's problem?

Answers: (i) Oh yes. (ii) Sadly not. (iii) Yes, I'm afraid. (iv) You will have to negotiate this one for yourself. (See all previous comments about breastfeeding vs. bottle-feeding.)

STATISTICS

According to one newspaper, a new father will lose, on average, 616 hours of sleep in the first three years. A new mother will lose 1,968 hours. These figures may or may not have been compiled by a new mother with a grievance.

OTHER PARENTS' LIES

'Oh yes, our Ethan sleeps through the night every night. Did so at three months.' These people are lying bastards, and you should never speak to them again.

CATNAPS

The only way I know to combat sleep deprivation. A parent who can put his/her head down for a 15-minute 'power nap' is a parent who might yet come out of this with sanity intact. I believe that all offices should be equipped with sofas for the use of sleep-deprived employees. Richer corporations should be prevailed upon to supply duvets and pillows. 15-minute alarm calls would also help. True, you always wake from a catnap with a vague sense of displacement and a tongue like old carpet, but after a cup of strong tea you will be as alert as a two-year-old.

For many fathers who spend the day loafing at so-called 'work', it should be relatively easy to arrange a schedule of health-restoring catnaps. But be careful that none of them exceeds 20 or 25 minutes, as then you go into a deeper sleep and can struggle to get over it. If you are unlucky enough to wake up after an hour, you will feel as though you are walking through treacle in a wetsuit and flippers carrying an oven in your rucksack. Slightly worse than usual, in other words.

FRESH AIR

In the early 1960s I myself was a baby and therefore frequently prambound. My parents were running a restaurant at the time and would leave me in my pram out on the street to be coochy-cooed at by old dears and jolly policemen. Only occasionally kidnapped and held for ransom, I continued to be thrust out on the pavement in all weathers, on the assumption that fresh air was intrinsically good for me, and would make me grow big or strong. Four decades later, I generally stay indoors as much as I can.

These days no babies are left out of doors unattended, but fresh air is still wonderfully good for baby, agree all the books and most grandmothers. Best of all is fresh air's fine record in getting recalcitrant babies to go to sleep. As they lie in their pram or pushchair, the waving of branches in the breeze first fascinates them, then hypnotises them, and eventually, if the gods of slumber are smiling upon you, anaesthetises them. A clear night sky can perform a similar function, which is why you so often see sad-eyed men propelling pushchairs around suburban streets at three in the morning. We have all been there. We have all been stopped by police officers wondering whether we were burglars. We have all been bundled into the backs of transit vans and beaten up by highly trained constables. It's a rite of passage for every dad.

Remember, though, that however bad things are for you, for someone else nearby they could be even worse. The man pushing baby around at three in the morning sees a car drive past. Behind the wheel is another sleep-deprived father. In the car seat, a gurgling infant chuckles evilly at the bags under his daddy's eyes. Father may have to drive a couple of miles before baby falls asleep. Or many, many more miles than that.

> *JEROME: The sleepless nights were unbelievable. She was colicky, and for three months didn't really sleep at all. I remember going out with her at night ... what was I doing? I'd read somewhere that a good thing to do with babies if they didn't sleep was to take them out. I remember taking her out for a walk round Wandsworth Common at one o'clock in the morning. She was crying away. Of course she was: it was so fucking cold. It certainly didn't work. Nothing did. So much of what we did was based on what we'd read. I took it as gospel, that this is what we ought to do. It was all just bollocks, really.*

TUNES

Babies *love* music. Most of the books recommend classical music, usually out of snobbery. True, pumping dance rhythms are not ideal for putting babies to sleep, but a lot of pop music can do the trick. Babies form tastes with indecent speed. My daughter always liked Leonard Cohen and Mark Knopfler of Dire Straits – maybe it was their croaky old voices. My son jiggled happily to anything with loud guitars and turned his tiny nose up at anything orchestral. I know of a baby that would fall asleep to Miles Davis but never to John Coltrane. Only one thing is for certain: whatever they like now, in twelve years they will be telling you it's shit, and listening to something else.

THATCHER

For years, she slept only four hours a night. Only now do you truly understand why she was as mad as a can of peas.

TIMES THE BABY WILL WAKE UP

- Moments after you get into bed to go to sleep.
- Later on in the night, moments after you have gone back to sleep after a lengthy interruption.
- 4.32 a.m.
- 5.46 a.m.
- During the day, just after your partner has walked out of the door.
- During your favourite TV programme.
- When you are on the phone.
- During sex.

TIMES THE BABY WON'T WAKE UP

- When you are washing up.
- When your partner is on the phone.
- Any other time you need the baby to be awake.

WHERE SHOULD BABY SLEEP?

Everyone wonders whether they are doing the right thing here. Some people have baby in bed with them. Half the books say this is the best thing you can do for baby. The other half say this is the worst thing you can do for baby. There are definite advantages. If baby wakes up, neither of you has to get out of bed. But if your baby is anything like mine, it will wriggle and flap for hours like a newly caught fish. You will live in terror of rolling over and squashing baby to death.[20] If baby is sleeping all night and you are not, obviously that's not ideal. You may come to the conclusion that having baby in bed with you is fine for the first few weeks, but more trouble than it's worth thereafter. Atrocious for the sex life, too.

Next option is the nursery. In all films and TV series in which someone has a baby, someone else lovingly decorates and equips a beautiful new nursery, complete with bunny rabbit wallpaper and roughly £3,000 worth of new toys. (The more carefully prepared the nursery, the higher the probability that the fictional baby will be pointlessly murdered, allowing its grieving parents several long scenes in the nursery sobbing over abandoned teddy bears.) Nurseries make parents feel that they are doing the right thing by their baby, and are good for showing off to neighbours. Nonetheless, a newborn baby may not react too favourably to being shoved away out of sight. Newborns want their mummies. They have no eye for interior decor. Proximity is all. Leave the nursery for later.

The standard compromise is to put the cot next to the bed in your room. This is convenient for whichever one will be feeding

---

20. Don't ask me why or how, but this *never* happens. Deborah Jackson, author of *Three In A Bed: The Benefits Of Sleeping With Your Baby*, says that 'the idea that co-sleeping is inherently dangerous for babies is an urban myth.'

Junior in the small hours, and also more convenient for the one who wants to go back to sleep. Baby can hear you breathing, if not snoring. If he/she wakes up, you can deal with the problem straight away with minimal fuss. All this makes baby feel secure and loved, which of course is the idea. It's not a bad compromise at all.

WIND

They guzzle, they digest, they burp and they fart. This is the theory. And yet their tiny digestive systems are fantastically sensitive – particularly at bedtime. Most babies go to sleep after they have been fed, but the air they inhale with their gutful of milk often wakes them again half an hour or so later. And a baby that has slept half an hour may not be quite as enthusiastic about going to sleep as it was half an hour ago. It may even have a spark of merriment in its eye. You, probably, will not.

So before you put Junior down for the night, you will need to wind him or her. One burp could do it. As the months pass you will learn to interpret every rumble and creak of your baby's digestive system. A few, rare babies fart and burp with ease; most seem to store them up, as though there's a shortage coming. So I have a tip, which I was told by a friend, who was told it by a friend, who said she saw it on TV. If your infant is full of wind, lean him/her against your shoulder and walk up and down the stairs over and over again. The up-and-down movement apparently encourages those tiny bubbles of gas to make straight for the exit. I know it works, because I did it several times a day for months on end for our firstborn, who was the Wind Queen of London N6. (I have never been so fit, before or since.)

Incidentally, breast milk is said by many experts to generate less wind than formula milk. I have read in another book that formula milk, because it is 'heavier', will satisfy babies more and therefore make them sleep longer. On your left, a rock. On your right, a hard place.

IT DOES GET BETTER

Desmond Morris in *Babywatching* reports that by the third week a 'typical' baby sleeps for 54 per cent of the daylight hours, compared with 71 per cent of the night-time. After six months the equivalent figures are 28 per cent for the daylight hours and 83 per cent for night-time. So instead of endless short bursts of sleep during day and night, Junior sleeps most of the night and is awake most of the day. Slowly he/she adjusts to normal human sleeping patterns. The daytime naps gradually merge into one fat morning nap and one fat afternoon nap. The light at the end of the tunnel may never get any closer, but at least it is there.

DREAMS

What are they dreaming about? A baby's REM sleep is wonderful to watch, for those few moments before your rank odour awakes the young package. What is going on behind those eyelids? Are they dreaming of running and jumping and other things they cannot do yet? Or of the womb, where they were warm and happy for all those months? No one will ever know. Personally, I think it's breasts.

IT IS ONLY A PHASE

Never forget this. However bad it gets, it is only ever a phase. Every child's sleep goes through countless different phases. Four- to five-year-olds, for instance, go through a nightmare phase, and can become quite fearful of the dark and of sleep itself. For a little baby the phases are briefer and more random. Maybe your baby is waking every night for no reason at 3.30. Not unnaturally, you deduce from this behaviour that he/she will wake every night at 3.30 between now and puberty. And then one night it stops. It was only a phase. It is *always* only a phase.

Tragically, this applies to the good phases as well. When your baby suddenly seems to crack the sleep habit, and kips throughout the night without interruption, the temptation is to crack open a bottle of something expensive. Resist this temptation. It is only a phase. In two weeks' time, baby will do something else completely: scream for no reason at midnight or wake at five fully refreshed. Realising that everything is only a phase protects you from the more crushing sleep-related disappointments.

TIREDNESS OLYMPICS

As the months pass, you and your partner will start to lose sympathy for each other's plight. So when one says 'Christ I feel tired,' the other will sigh grumpily and/or say 'Well, I'm tired, too.' These are the Tiredness Olympics, an ongoing competition so called because they last four years. My girlfriend was always tireder and more miserable than I was. When forced to get up, even though it was her turn, her sighs would virtually strip the duvet from the bed. And as sympathy dies, so your determination to exert your human rights becomes stronger. If it was my turn for the lie-in, nuclear war wouldn't shift me. Worst sound in the world: crying child. Second worst sound: grunt of pleasure from partner going back to sleep moments after you have got up to answer worst sound in the world. Come to think of it, they may be first equal.

RESILIENCE

Adrenalin and the novelty of it all keep you going at the start. You surprise yourself; a new gear of competence seems to kick in. Parenthood is like any emergency: human beings somehow rise to it. Although you feel atrocious, you manage to do everything that is required of you. You have no energy for anything else, such as work or a social life, but that's normal. As Libby Purves says, 'for a few months after a birth, nobody should expect much beyond survival and the odd quiet drink in front of the television.' (Television? Pah! She had it easy.)

But this resilience is a scarce resource. Once used up, it does not come back. Waking up even once in the night when your baby is a year old may take more out of you than waking three times a night nine months before. You are like a rubber band which has lost its boing. It gets worse with a second child, even though by then you know what you are doing and can avoid making the same imbecilic mistakes you made last time. But the resilience has gone. These days, one bad night can take me three days to get over. And if there's another bad night in those three days ...

> *HARVEY: The big thing I didn't reckon on was the continuing loss of sleep. Not just in the baby years, but all the years afterwards. It would seem to me, as a trained biologist, that small children share a large part of their DNA with the cockerel. As a teenager I vividly recall marvelling at my father's ability to rise at some ungodly hour every morning and appear in my bedroom with a cup of tea. After two children of my own, I now know how he managed it. Year after year of early rising – and my brother and I were the reason for it.*

18 the blues, the love, the fear

Have we talked about 'emotional rollercoasters' yet? Everyone does. At the end of the day people who write parenthood books love a cliché. So do parents: when your brain keeps sputtering and conking out at random, you don't really want to be looking for fresh new ways of saying 'emotional rollercoaster'. Especially as it describes rather succinctly what both fathers and mothers go through during pregnancy, the birth and the first few months thereafter. Pregnancy is the queue for the emotional roller-coaster. You stand around for ages, eating junk food and becoming increasingly bad-tempered. 'Everyone has to queue,' says your partner soothingly. At last you get on the ride (the first contractions). It starts slowly, creaking up that long, steep slope. It seems to take forever. You are locked in; you cannot escape. Halfway through your ascent, the engineers down below change shifts.

But just as you were on the verge of giving up hope, you reach the top of the slope. There is a moment of silence. A sharp chill in the air. An overwhelming sense of impending doom. You hear the first screams from other passengers. (Or is that you?) And then the descent into hell. Up and down, in and out, over and over and over again. Your wallet falls out of your pocket. It's money you will never see again. You think you might throw up. Why on earth did you eat curry last night? You knew you would be going on the emotional rollercoaster today. But up it surges, like a bilious tsunami, out of your mouth and straight onto the back of the head of the person sitting in front. Who is also you, by some unpleasant relativistic coincidence. Your partner looks at you in disgust, wondering why she chose you and not 1,750 other men who had far better credentials.

There, sadly, the analogy fails. Real rollercoasters only last a minute or so, and many people enjoy them so much they want to go straight back on again. Whereas only an idiot would contemplate a second ride on the emotional rollercoaster. At least for a couple of years, or until Junior starts school.

And that is assuming they can ever get off the bloody thing. Some emotional rollercoasters seem to go on indefinitely. Up and down, in and out, over and over and over again. Who would have thought that one man could throw up that many times?

THE BLUES

Hooray for endorphins. These delightful little hormones mimic the effects of morphine and help blunt your perception of pain and stress. The brain produces endorphins on an industrial scale during pregnancy and childbirth, and without them the mother of your child would surely go barking mad. But as soon as baby is out in the world and filling 60 nappies a week, her endorphin levels drop sharply. The result is baby blues, the almost universal realisation that this motherhood business is not quite what it was cracked up to be. Most mothers go into a bit of a decline in the weeks after the birth. They are exhausted, they are recovering from physical trauma and the bloody baby won't stop crying. They may be struggling to cope with the practicalities of parenthood. They may want to give the baby back before the 28-day warranty is up. Thanks, I've tried it, but I don't think this is for me. There must be loads of people out there who wouldn't mind looking after a slightly used baby. What do you mean, there isn't a 28-day warranty? Do you need all the original packaging? We've got the placenta, if that's any help.

The main problem with baby blues is that many mothers don't realise, or acknowledge, that they have them. They just think they are failing to cope. Or they may find the term 'baby blues' so insufferably cutesy – I haven't been able to trace it, but I feel sure that it's American – that they simply refuse to suffer from them. No one wants to be diagnosed with a euphemism. It sounds like the sort of thing the Care Bears would have. Calling something 'baby blues' is a licence for doctors not to take it seriously, and many of them don't. Here are some anti-depressants. Now piss off.

Nonetheless, a small proportion of those suffering baby blues descend further into the torment of full-blooded postnatal depression.[21] This is nasty. If your beloved moves into PND territory, she will need all your love and support to get out of it. Signs to look out for include: heightened anxiety; irrational fears; insomnia; loss of appetite; tendency to stay in pyjamas all day; loss of proportion; withdrawal from the world; feelings of inadequacy and helplessness; strange glint in eye when she looks at kitchen knives; screams like banshee whenever she sees baby. In other words, if she is obviously bonkers, then chances are she has postnatal depression.

How you react is important. Try not to say things like 'Pull yourself together' or 'Snap out of it'. No jury would convict her for your bloody and prolonged murder. Instead, talk to her, listen to her, look after her, cook for her, be there for her. Make sure she is not by herself all the time, even if you are at work for the usual life-saving chunks of daylight. Go to the doctor for her if she won't go for herself. Remember, postnatal depression is only temporary. Either she gets better or it becomes normal depression because it is no longer immediately postnatal. There is always a solution, even if it does not solve anything.

The really scary one is postnatal psychosis. (Has anyone made a film about this yet?) It is said to affect only one in a

21. Everyone says ten to 15 per cent, but I don't know where these figures come from. They could be the result of years of meticulous research by dedicated medical personnel, or a wild guess formulated with the help of a pin.

thousand women, but that seems rather a lot to me. Signs to look out for include: sleeping all day; crying all day; tense, nervous headache; phases of manic jollity; paranoia; hallucinations; occasional tendency to stand on roofs with baby and threaten to jump. This is the very sharp end of postnatal depression, requiring instant medical treatment and, usually, hospitalisation. If the 1 in 1,000 figure is correct, it means that 20 mothers go completely mad for every one baby that is born with Down's syndrome. I don't know about you, but I'm not sure I wanted to know that.

Incidentally, even if she does manage to avoid the baby blues, she will still find herself crying uncontrollably on the fourth or fifth day after the birth. This is completely normal, happens to everyone, and has nothing to do with the fact that she has just realised that the baby looks like you.

THE BLUES (II)

But how about the father? Can't he feel miserable too?

Mothers have baby blues, postnatal depression and postnatal psychosis. Fathers do well to have a hangover. There simply isn't the same level of sympathy for our plight. My informal researches, however, suggest that far more men than is known about experience some level of postnatal depression. We are not unfeeling monsters, much as we pretend otherwise. As was proved in earlier emergencies, we are more typically the strong but silent type. But the Gary Cooper and Clint Eastwood templates are of little use when faced with a tiny screaming baby. Clint, of course, dealt with an orang utan in two of his more pathetic films. But I don't remember ever seeing him with an infant tucked under his arm. 'Shoot first, ask questions later' is advice best unheeded by fathers of small children, although when you start going to parent-and-toddler groups you might be sorely tempted. Most men struggle with their feelings on some level; but even the touchiest and feeliest of New Men can hit the depths after childbirth. The reasons just stack up.

- Loss of freedom. Required to stay in every night. Leisure time obliterated.
- Tired of dealing with partner. Miserable fat cow always eating cakes and crying. She wanted bloody baby in first place. Unable to say these things to her face.
- Financial burden of new role. Had been planning to buy flash car and go on expensive holidays. Now destined for penury and estate car. Partner no longer working.[22] No hope of situation ever improving.
- Lack of support. Friends no use. Family worse. Everyone supporting doughnut-addled partner, no one helping you.
- Possible lingering resentment over treatment at hospital. Obliged to watch horrors of birth without feeling part of it. Experience hard to process, let alone get over. Trauma sits in pit of stomach, festering.

---

22. Only 16 per cent of mothers return to full-time work in the first three years. Another 33 per cent do part-time work, which means half of all new mothers give up work altogether. Most new dads, then, will be their household's main or sole breadwinner. And cakewinner.

- Baby doesn't seem worth it. Small ugly thing. Looks exactly like you.
- Partner obsessed with baby, has no time for you. Has made it clear that you have done your job and can now whistle if you suggest renewing sexual relations.
- Tired. Oh, so tired.

All things considered, it is remarkable that both of you are not standing on the roof threatening to jump. I know I am.

> *DUNCAN: She was a difficult baby, she was hard work all the way through. She was always screaming and crying, and life was hell for the first six months, it really was. When you're going through that you wonder why anyone would ever want to be a parent. And you understand why people throw their children out of the window on the forty-eighth floor. Seems quite a rational thing to do at half past three in the morning when you've got to be up at six to go to work.*
>
> *ANTHONY: I didn't get the baby blues, but Astrid did. Lots of reasons, too complex to go into now; and it wasn't recognised for a very long time. It took years for her to get any help; she finally got some before our second was born; it was partial but helpful. She got the blues too after the second, but is really fighting it now, and is getting some constructive help. I've found it really hard to deal with. But there's lots of good stuff going on with Astrid and she's incredibly brave embracing the whole mum thing. One consequence of her being off work at the*

> *moment is that we're just totally broke. And that puts a monkey on your back you don't need. I never want R to grow up as I did, always being told there's not enough of anything. Even if we're broke he's going to be told there's plenty (of love and fun if not fancy toys).*

Quite how you deal with all this I don't know. All the experts say, Think positively. Great. Just what you need to be told. If you could think positively, you wouldn't be miserable. It's like telling a cat to stop miaowing.

All I can suggest to fathers is, try to bond with the baby. At the heart of many fathers' postnatal depression is a feeling of detachment from the whole process, which itself may come from a feeling of detachment from the baby. Fathers who instantly click with their babies seem to be immune from the nastier manifestations of PND, while those who look upon this tiny stranger with disgust and/or the obscure feeling that they have somehow been conned are most vulnerable. The fact is, the baby is here to stay; it is going nowhere. Fathers are more mobile. Men are more likely to leave the marital home in the first three months after the birth of their first child than at any other time. It seems reasonable to assume that most, if not all, of these fleeing dads have some form of PND. If anyone even acknowledged this, let alone tried to help, maybe fewer would leave. But when you are depressed, one notion you simply cannot accommodate is that things will get better. One of the main themes of this book, I hope, is that things do get better. Eventually. If you stick it out. And then one day it dawns on you that fatherhood is a good thing, that it's worth all the sleeplessness and the endless cooking of pasta and the agonising lack of sex. That you wouldn't be without this child, or (in time and with luck) these children. Which brings us neatly onto ...

THE LOVE

Mothers are, to a greater or lesser extent, hard-wired to love their infants. Fathers are not. A few of us – and I think we can justly call them 'lucky bastards' – fall instantly in love with their new babies, as though floodlights have been switched on. I can't say this happened to me, and I don't think it's as common as people think. This indifference, or apathy, or absence of something you expected as of right, may come as a disappointment, and not just to you. Your partner may be enraged. She may think that it is only you who has not fallen in love at first sight with your progeny, that it is your specific, individual failure, and possibly further proof of your fundamental worthlessness. Not that she will say any of this, because she is too busy cooing over the baby, but her eyes will say it, and so will her body language. Mothers are also hard-wired to identify totally with their babies. Love me, love my baby.

You can see why so many new dads run. Who needs any of this? But love does come, in time. It's a strange and wondrous thing, impossible to explain. Gradually, this infant intruder creeps into your affections. The floodlights are turned on, but they are on an unfeasibly slow dimmer switch, over which you have no control. As babies are learning to live, so their fathers are learning to love. And the strangest aspect of all this is that the love does not seem to be at the expense of anything.

Think of your life as a view out of the window. Your vista represents everything that you do and enjoy, your friends, your pleasures, your life. When a baby comes along you assume that some of this vista will simply disappear, to be replaced by baby. There isn't room in the vista for everything you used to enjoy. You have read that a new dad will give up 2,200 hours in pubs and restaurants in the first 16 years of his child's life. The bright colours of fun will be blotted out by the drab grey clouds of parental responsibility.

And for the first few weeks, as baby cries and cries and your partner seems to turn into a different person and you seem unable to feel anything for the baby more positive than mild curiosity, this is the way your vista will be. But baby knows better. Baby needs father to love it; baby looks up lovingly at father; father begins to fall in love. And the vista of your life suddenly expands. You are looking out of a bigger window now, and one of the supporting walls may have been taken away. Emotionally, at least, baby has replaced nothing. Baby has added something, and will go on adding more. Your life will be richer for knowing baby, and you realise that life without baby would now be poorer than anything you would be willing to tolerate. The vista opens out, and those clouds are not as drab or grey as you first thought. Without realising it, let alone understanding it, you have made the transition. Now you really are a father. Congratulations. Welcome to the club.

FERGUS: Took me six months to fall in love with them. Each time. I think it's to do with the end of breastfeeding. Because you then start having more of a role. And I've actually been very involved as a father, much more than most. Because I take them to school and I put them to bed. I like feeling involved. And it was the feeling that I was part of it that I think made me feel happy with it.

When the second one stopped breastfeeding, we were on holiday in Greece. It was the first time I'd had sole control of her. And I took her in a backpack up this mountain. And we got lost. I ended up climbing up this sheer slope, this scree, feeling this total sense of panic – you know, the first day I look after her, I manage to kill her. And the fear for her suddenly kick-started this incredible feeling of love for her. And also this desire on my part to make sure she didn't die, didn't get eaten by wolves or something like that. And suddenly I realised I had a role, even though it was my fault that we were in such a ridiculous position. It was my fault and it was my job to get her out of there.

IVAN: I think when the child is born you feel protective and loving, but there was a moment when I realised that I loved W, that he was just this precious, precious thing to me. He was born in July and my mum died suddenly in November. We had her funeral the week after W's christening. We'd gone around to her house to sort out some effects and I think this was about a month after she died, and people had been saying, he doesn't seem to be affected by his mother's death. I think people were expecting me to crack up, and I didn't. And there was one particular occasion when I was with W at her house, and he was by a sofa or something, and he fell over, and clonked his head, and he was only about four or five months old, and you think, oh Christ, he's hit his head, and you whip him up to the hospital, and of course he was absolutely fine. But I was so distraught at the thought that my carelessness might have hurt him. In the car park at the hospital I just completely went to pieces, and all this crap about my mother suddenly came out. I'd never cried like that before, or since, it was horrible. And it was at that point that you suddenly realise that this small bundle is so astonishingly precious, and you love it to bits.

I think the surge of love you feel for your children is unlike anything you would feel for an adult. Babies have been designed by evolution to make you love them. Soon you will be carrying photos of them, which is about as sad as it gets.

And it has nothing to do with whether you like babies as babies. If you happen to regard all other children as squirming, shouty, self-indulgent, over-pampered little gits, then you are probably a normal well-adjusted British male. Other people's children can be repulsive. It is only your own that are uncommonly clever, charming and pleasing on the eye. Mothers, more naturally diplomatic, can pretend to like other people's children and even get on with them *in extremis*. No one expects fathers to do this. No one shows us photos of their awful, dull children. They wouldn't dare.

Here is a strange thing, unearthed by Desmond Morris in his fascinating book *Babywatching*. If you look at something or someone you like, your pupils dilate, even in the brightest of light. If it is something or someone you don't like, your pupils contract. In Morris's experiment, people were shown a beautiful, grinning, non-crying baby in the business of being adorable. Most women, whether or not they had children of their own, showed a marked positive response. Their pupils dilated; they liked the look of the baby. Men who had had children also responded positively. But men who hadn't had children evinced a strong negative response. Some pretended otherwise, but their contracting pupils told their truth: they hated the little bleeder. Morris's conclusion is intriguing. He says that women come 'ready-primed for maternal behaviour', while men must have their instincts activated by going through parenthood themselves. In other words, their vista needs to expand. For men this could be how you define 'growing up'. No wonder so many of us seek to put it off as long as possible.

THE FEAR

And once you have learned to love them, The Fear sets in. This is the monstrous and irrational terror that something unspecifically awful is going to happen to your baby. You have come so far with Junior. You don't want to lose him/her now. Suddenly the world seems a dreadfully hostile place. Around every corner, paedophiles. In the next road, a car that is about to run your child down. In the air, killer microbes. In the food, killer microbes. You look at your neighbours in a new light. The bloke a few doors down the road, who looks a bit odd. Supposing he is a bit odd? Supposing he is exceptionally odd? Unless you get a grip of yourself, every smiling granny can seem like a serial killer, and before you know it, you are putting grilles on windows and electrifying doorknobs. The Fear does this to people.

As men, of course, we like to think of ourselves as rational beings, and therefore more immune to emotional excesses than the mad women we all seem to live with. If only it were so. Once the small person has crept into your affections you too will feel the lurking terror in your stomach, or wherever terror chooses to lurk in your anatomy. And then it stays there. The Fear mutates regularly. It never leaves. Here's a rough timetable of the misery to come:

- First six months: cot death. This is much rarer than it used to be, thanks to recent and well-distributed advice on how to avoid it (essentially this boils down to making sure your child sleeps on its back and doesn't overheat). But a few babies still die unexplained deaths before the age of six months, and probably always will. As a result, all parents live in constant fear of this happening. Bear in mind that it almost certainly won't, although this is unlikely to stop either of you from going in to check that Junior is still alive 15 minutes after you last checked. All that time and effort spent getting your baby to sleep, and then you go in and check and inadvertently wake him/her up. It's The Fear, you know.

- From two months: the vaccination horror. The MMR controversy rumbles on, and may survive us all. No one wants an autistic child; no one wants their child to die of measles; and are all these vaccinations good for an infant immune system anyway? You can read every piece of literature on the subject. You can make a decision based on probabilities rather than certainties. You can cross your fingers and not walk under ladders, which was my response to the problem. Most of us feel adrift. It's The Fear, you know.

- Later on: traffic, meningitis, odd neighbours, insane bus drivers mowing down queues of waiting pedestrians at bus stops, drugs, sex, organophosphates, saucepans of boiling water, smoking, rare but newsworthy childhood diseases, pollution, electric shocks, TV violence, tattoos, body-piercing, atrocious music, Kentucky Fried Chicken. As the journalist Barbara Ellen put it, 'Whatever the situation, whatever the weather, whatever the age of your child, The Fear is always there – your own black cloud dragged along on the end of a dog lead.' Which reminds me: I forgot dogs, which can maul your little ones. And dogshit, which can blind them. The list has no end.

Every new parent doubts their own competence. We are always imagining the worst. Carry baby down the stairs, and think, what if I drop her down the stairs? Take him into a shop, and think, what if I leave him in the shop and he is taken by loons? The anxiety is never ending.

> *CLIFF: My wife was constantly fretting that something was wrong, reading books, particularly by some woman ... Penelope Leach. Penelope bloody Leach. Ah, she made our lives hell.*

So my wife regularly thought that, for instance, that bump in the head shouldn't be like that, that there was something seriously wrong. And, of course, I spent my whole time trying to assuage these fears but without any knowledge whatsoever. So I was worried that I was the one stopping our child getting the life-saving operation, or whatever. I remember lots of these sorts of things. And being woken up not only by the baby but by my wife worrying about things. It just seemed to be one incessant worry.

ANTHONY: Couldn't sleep for the first few months, 'cause I was convinced someone would come in the night and steal R. Used to sit up like a caveman in the moonlight, checking out every bang and knock and nightly noise.

And specific circumstances generate new, specific fears. We followed all the advice for our firstborn about cot deaths. No smoking – which wasn't too hard, as neither of us smoked in the first place. We didn't give her a pillow, or swaddle her with 17 duvets, and we put her down to sleep on her back, as recommended by everyone in the world. The only trouble was, she wouldn't go to sleep on her back. So we tried her on her side, which is the next best option. It didn't work. After weeks of misery, we took a deep breath and did the worst thing any parent can do, according to experts: we put her to sleep on her front. Every night, as she drifted happily off to sleep in the Death Position, we waited for the doorbell to ring and the hooded man with the scythe to come in. We dared not mention what we had done to other parents, in case they rang up social services. A few of our best friends knew, but they thought we were taking the most terrible risk – akin, perhaps, to putting your child to sleep every night on the hard shoulder of a six-lane motorway. Needless to say, she survived. Two and a half years later our son was born, and he did exactly the same. And we did exactly the same. And exactly the same thing happened. Nothing.

Not that I am suggesting that you should tempt fate with your children's lives. Sudden Infant Death Syndrome (SIDS), as cot death is clinically known, is as ghastly a thing as can happen to a family. My point is that the probabilities are always smaller than we acknowledge. Just as a baby is almost certain not to be born with spina bifida, so your child is extremely unlikely to die a cot death. Around 200 British babies do each year, which represents 0.2 per cent of babies born. And many of the higher risk factors almost certainly won't apply to you. As well as smoking, these include drug use, maternal alcoholism and social isolation. According to the British Confidential Enquiry into Stillbirths and Deaths In Infancy, sleeping in the same room as your small baby is 'strongly protective' against cot death. This includes sleeping in the same bed: in cotless cultures in Africa, Asia and South America, cot death is unheard of.

You would never guess this from some of the newspaper headlines. 'Perils Of Babies In Parent's Bed' and 'Adult Bed No Place For Babies' were two I saw one month last year, stories based on some wonderfully shaky statistics from the US. Newspapers are more responsible than anyone for fuelling The Fear. And providing a lot of their raw material are American researchers and interest groups. In July 2003 a group of US paediatricians identified a new risk to babies being put to sleep on their backs, as cot death guidelines now recommend. True, these babies may be more likely to survive those crucial first months, but up to 48 per cent may find that on their first birthday they have flattened heads. (Note: 'up to' 48 per cent. This could easily mean two per cent.) To correct this condition, say these eminent paediatricians and plastic surgeons, could cost $3,000. A nice way to drum up business.

And it gets better. More research has revealed that putting babies to sleep only on their backs 'has raised a generation of infants who risk never learning, or learning very belatedly, how to crawl ... There was even the suggestion that [they] would struggle with their handwriting and motor skills when at school if urgent corrective action – placing them on their tummies – was not taken.'[23] We live in a world in which putting your child on its stomach has become 'urgent corrective action'. (The solution, obvious surely to all, has already been christened 'tummy time'.)

As your child grows and you, too, become obsessed with paedophiles, bear in mind the often-ignored fact inconvenient to all tabloid newspapers and vigilante groups: no more children are abducted and/or killed by lunatics than 50 years ago, a hundred years ago, or ever. Indeed, the homicide rate for school-age girls is lower than for *any* group in society (including boys of the same age). But The Fear is at work, stoked by excessively violent films and TV series. Result: children's freedoms are

23. Esther Addley in the *Guardian*.

unnecessarily curtailed, and parents go loopy. For some The Fear is a life sentence. Franklin D. Roosevelt, when he had already been elected President of the United States, and his mother was over 80, let slip that he had never in his whole life gone outdoors without the old bag calling after him, 'Franklin! Are you sure you're dressed warmly enough?' There's something of Ma Roosevelt in us all, whether we admit it or not.

19
registered dad

Within the first 40 days parents are required to register their baby's birth. This is easily dealt with. To find out where your nearest Registrar of Births is, phone your local council or ask your midwives. If you are married, only one of you needs to go along. If you are not, you must both be there in glowing Technicolor. Three other things you need to remember: (a) your passports, (b) your hospital paperwork and (c) your baby. The registrar will look carefully at the first two and slightly more fleetingly at the third. Does baby have your ears? And her nose? Really, the registrar couldn't care less. It's his day off tomorrow and he can't decide whether to go fishing or visit prostitutes. Within the blink of an eye the significant forms are filled in and, for a small fee, you get a birth certificate and the reassuring feeling that your baby is now officially alive.

It also means that you are now a Registered Dad. If at some time in the future you are savagely murdered by lunatics or injured in a wholly preventable train crash, newspapers will refer to you as a 'father-of-one'. By creating life you have unwittingly become a person of consequence. You are a parent. According to many people's prejudices, that makes you a pillar of the community. From there it's but a short step to fat bastard, pompous old fool and desperate, pitiable dirty old man.

Still, all communities need their pillars, if only to chop them down. In your new role you will do many things you could never have imagined doing before all this crept up on you. These include:

- Going out to the shops to buy Tupperware.
- Willingly going to bed at 9.30 in the evening.
- Eyeing up women as potential mothers as well as bed partners.
- Waiting at a pedestrian crossing until the light goes green instead of nipping across when there's a break in the traffic.
- Sticking your nose right up against your child's arse to check whether or not there's a poo in there.

(This latter one is best performed in public places, for the satisfying reactions you'll receive from passers-by. All women will approve; some may even tell you to your face. Several men won't even notice, because they do the same thing every day themselves. Others will grimace or retch. They are not man enough to inhale closely from a baby's bum. You are.)

You may also spend some time wondering exactly what it

means to you to be a father. At this stage, mothers are generally too sore and exhausted to think too much about being a mother. Being women, they have been thinking about it for years, anyway. They have also endured nine months of pregnancy, which tends to concentrate the mind wonderfully. Whereas most of us spend that time not thinking about anything at all if we can help it. It is the fate of fathers always to be slightly behind the game. Walking down the street, we wonder whether we are walking in a slightly more, well, fatherly way. Is there such a thing? Do people treat you differently? Do you feel different?

If so, that's probably as it should be. Remarkably, given the increased incidence of postnatal depression among fathers, all the research shows that becoming a father can actually do wonders for your self-esteem. You look in the mirror in the morning and think, Hey! you're all right. No, you're better than all right. You're a-fucking-mazing. (Make sure you are only thinking this rather than saying it out loud.)

In the long run, you may be surprised and pleased to hear, fathers seem to do rather well out of family life. Studies show that, while women often feel equivocal about motherhood, fatherhood just makes men happier. That patina of seriousness you always lacked; well, you've got it now. And then there's the most fundamental truth of all: your equipment works. You have *cojones*. The proof lives with you and probably has your surname. This knowledge is a wonderful thing, and the glorious smugness that now resides in your manly chest is something that, you will be delighted to hear, time will never erode, not even a little bit.

Most mothers won't care to hear any of this. As far as they are concerned, you always had the easier share of the pregnancy, in that you did nothing at all. Now that the baby is born, chances are that she is stuck at home, greasy-haired with stress and rage, while you swan off to work every morning, for what she regards as a jolly day out. If you are the sole breadwinner, as many men are, it does not matter that you have to worry about money or accommodation or the increasing likelihood that you will get sacked because your work is so poor because you never get any sleep at night. Your partner's eyes will glaze over long before you finish explaining. The following morning she will sit in a café eating cakes with other new mothers and they will ask each other, with sighs of infinite weariness, 'What use are fathers anyway?'

WELL, WHAT USE ARE FATHERS ANYWAY?

That is a very good question and I am very pleased you have asked it.

GO ON.

Yes, I am very pleased you have asked it, it being a very good question.

THANK YOU, BUT DO YOU INTEND TO ANSWER IT AT SOME POINT?

I'd love to. But we fathers sometimes have a problem justifying our existence, beyond the obvious roles of provider, uncomplaining domestic slave, chauffeur and reader of bedtime stories with copious use of silly voices. Lesbians solved the problem decades ago with a turkey baster – so efficiently, in fact, that turkey basters now need a new name, as virtually no one uses them to baste turkeys any more. (Heterosexual women use them only to wield at their menfolk, while saying things like 'This would be more use than you are.') The absolute uselessness of men generally, and fathers specifically, has become a cornerstone of our popular culture, assumed to be true of us all unless we can individually prove otherwise. The Maternity Alliance – which sounds a terrifying organisation, possibly paramilitary in outlook – published a useful pamphlet in 2000 called *And Baby Makes Three: A Man's Guide To Becoming A Father*. 'It is hard to find media portrayals ... that are heroic about fathers,' it said, accurately. 'Instead you get a load of unimpressive stereotypes:

- fathers work too hard and neglect their children.
- fathers abandon their families and refuse to pay maintenance.
- fathers are too ham-fisted to change a nappy properly.
- fathers are distant, uncaring authority figures.
- fathers are people with comic dress sense who like pottering in garden sheds.
- fathers are like big kids: another person for the mother to look after.'

This makes depressing reading for men, although being men, we all have to tot up and see how many of them apply to us. I declare here that none of them apply to me, although I admit

I'd probably score one out of six if I possessed a garden shed.[24] My girlfriend says I score two out of six with or without the shed. Thinking back a generation, I realise that my father scored an easy three, so however you look at it, I represent an improvement.

But it's never as simple as that. If these old-fashioned notions of fatherhood now seem ridiculous, what has replaced them can inspire even fiercer hostility. The touchy-feely New Man stereotype gives many of us the collywobbles, partly because it seems to represent someone so in touch with their feminine side that their masculine side has disappeared completely. This is the sort of man who will have willingly put on an Empathy Belly when his partner was pregnant.[25] He will have been *brilliant* at the birth, massaging her shoulders until his thumbs had worn down to stumps, and taking her abuse on the chin without complaint. I hate him and I want to kick him, and so do most of the fathers I spoke to, even if he doesn't actually exist.

Where is the truth in all this? In October 2002 the Equal Opportunities Commission published a report in which it neatly divided British fathers into four distinct categories. Enforcer Dad is the old-fashioned stereotype: he sets the rules, but is not involved in day-to-day care. Enforcer Dad shouts a lot and, in

---

24. Don't knock garden sheds. The chorus of XTC's song 'Fruit Nut' (from their *Apple Venus Vol. 1* album) is 'Every man needs a shed to keep him sane'.

25. Briefly in vogue in the early 1990s, the Empathy Belly was a great lump of something you strapped around your waist so that you found out just what pregnancy was like. As well as putting pressure on your abdomen and bladder, and wrecking your back muscles, it also simulated foetal kicking movements. Arnold Schwarzenegger wore something like it for the film *Junior*.

nineteenth-century novels, wore a black frock coat. He kisses his children only on birthdays and Christmas Day and even then reluctantly, as he would rather 'toughen them up'. Enforcer Dad's dad was an Enforcer Dad – but I think you already knew that.

Category Two is Entertainer Dad, who is good at amusing the kids but useless at everything else. Does not help around the house, avoids having to discipline anyone, but great fun at parties, to which he wears a revolving bow-tie. Most mothers want Entertainer Dad killed, and may hire someone to do it.

Then we have Useful Dad, who does his bit domestically and regularly looks after the kids, but always defers to the authority of his partner. He sees himself as helping her out, rather than taking responsibility for things himself. The Equal Opportunities Commission nearly approves of Useful Dad, but not quite.

Finally, there is Fully Involved Dad, who is 'equally involved in running the home and family,' says the report. He does more than his fair share of everything, can cook to cordon bleu standard and is dynamite in the sack, with the fingers of a concert pianist, a tongue that could lift weights and the lung control of an Olympic swimmer. The EOC likes Fully Involved Dad a lot. The rest of us are going round to his house now to kick him.

What a choice! Any father reading this rubbish would become profoundly depressed, although in reality most of us combine all these stereotypes in various proportions. We are all probably a combination of Entertainer and Useful, and little though we may wish to admit it, have a smidgen of Fully Involved too. We are Slightly Fully Involved. I suspect you have to be a bit touchy-feely if you are going to be any good at fathering. Most of us probably are, naturally and spontaneously, without thinking about it. We are all New Men now, after a fashion.

YOU STILL HAVEN'T ANSWERED MY QUESTION

Yes, impressive, isn't it? But it isn't an easy one to answer. We can see clearly what the mother is for. She is likely to be what social workers call 'the primary carer'. She has these breasts which solve 90 per cent of known infancy problems. She seems to have nurturing instincts that most men, quite simply, lack. We have to learn everything, and however hard we try we never seem to be quite there. This can be hugely frustrating. As men we are used to being at the centre of everything, so to be shoved out here on the margins, watching our child's earliest weeks and months at one remove, can be dispiriting, not to mention demotivating. More often that not, the arrival of a child drastically reduces family income, so the father finds himself working harder to make up the difference. Gravity weakens the further you are away from an object. And as the father drifts off, in some cases never to be seen again, the newly single mother says, 'What use are fathers anyway?'

I am not going to demonise single mothers. Frightened and angry people do this already in certain newspapers. My mother was a single mother for a while; my girlfriend's mother was a single mother for rather longer. They are both splendid and impressive people, for whom life has at times been a struggle. They would rather not have been single mothers – not because society might disapprove (who cares about that?), but because ɪg us and our siblings up was grindingly hard work. As if it's ̣ot tough enough for two parents. But this is my point: if the father has any function at all, it is to Be There. Looking after a baby *is* grindingly hard work, and it helps if there is more than one person around to do it. Simply by taking part do you justify your existence.

It is easy to lose sight of this. You are at work all day, you come home, the baby is screaming and the place is a sty. Your partner expects you to muck in immediately, not because she is unreasonable (although she may very well be) but because she is knackered and desperately needs some time off. The daily transition you must make from work life (ordered, remunerated) to domestic life (chaotic, cripplingly expensive) is a difficult one to handle, not just for you but for your partner as well. It can become a flashpoint of pent-up resentment. Don't be surprised by this. Even the most easy-going men struggle to adjust to the sheer mundanity of childcare. A lot of it is catastrophically dull. Mothers have more hours in the day to get used to it, but that doesn't mean they do. There have been several books recently by writer-mothers, all of them highly intelligent and accomplished women, who have clearly loathed the relentless treadmill of parenthood. It may be that the cleverest and most career-oriented women find it most difficult to adjust to the drudgery of it all. My girlfriend, who is also highly intelligent and accomplished, nonetheless believes you need to have a certain in-built bovine quality to get the most out of it. Although this could be her way of explaining why, when breastfeeding our two, she so often went 'Moo.'

Something similar applies to fathers. I think the only way you can make sense of the drudgery is to surrender to it completely. Because it does not last forever, and your children will be happier and more secure when they are older if you have Been There, doing what needs to be done. Once you surrender to it, you might not actually enjoy it, but you won't resent it as much, either. Sometimes you are barely aware of it. Just the other day I realised that I had wiped three arses in the preceding 15 minutes, only one of them my own.

Human babies, of course, need more parental care than any other species: this is a direct consequence of our awesome evolutionary success. Other primates have only maternal care, but somewhere along the line humans started to fall in love, or 'pair-bond' as anthropologists would have it, and so paternal care became available, too. Our children simply need a lot of looking after, and a mother can only do so much. When we all lived in tribes there was an extended family to help out. No longer, of course. Grandparents, increasingly, are on the other side of the country, if not the other side of the world. You could almost say that we have evolved to a point at which fathers are more important than ever before, not less important.

Two parents of different sexes also supply a certain variety. Men and women are different. Women have observed this empirically and men have proved it scientifically. So having one of each around the house means a full set of gender role models from whom the child can learn how to live its life. Here's a strange but, I think, fascinating example. Mothers, in the earliest weeks of new life, tend to carry or sit holding their baby face to face. Fathers, by contrast, usually hold the baby so that it is facing out into the world. Subconsciously, say psychologists, the father sees it as his job to introduce the baby to the world. Most men do this without realising. It is one instinct we do not have to learn.

Your primary function is to Be There. It may not sound like much but it is too much for some. In the USA, whose social trends we tend to follow as though index-linked, 36 per cent of children live apart from their biological fathers. Of these, 40 per cent haven't seen those fathers in a year or more. We now know that children brought up by one parent are more likely as they grow up to do badly at school, suffer from depression, commit crimes. This isn't necessarily because single mothers are no good at their job; it's because the father-shaped hole in a young life can be difficult, even impossible, to fill.

So if you do look in the mirror from time to time and think, 'Mm. You're OK,' that is no bad thing, and it may even be true. As one recent academic book on the subject put it, with unacademic pithiness, 'Parenting is an ordinary everyday activity, and yet it is also one of the most skilled, difficult and demanding tasks an adult is called upon to perform.' You might as well give yourself credit for this, as no one else will.

20
the six-month audit

The first months of parenthood can pass in a bit of a fug. 'Fug off,' you shout at your partner after a particularly bad night. Meanwhile, the infant continues to grow and develop at an alarming rate.

One month old: can hold its head up about an inch when lying on stomach.

Two months: can lift its head to 45 degrees when on stomach. Otherwise, still as floppy as an inadequately stuffed soft toy.

Three months: can lift shoulders. And turn its head when it hears your voice, and express pleasure by waving arms and kicking legs. Can keep head up steadily now for a few seconds.

Four months: can sit up. But only if you put it in the sitting position and hold it there. Can also cross its feet, and will start reaching for its toes. Which are currently too far away.

Five months: can push up on its arms for about a second and

a half. Then clump! hits the floor and bursts into tears. Also starting to put things in its mouth. Full control of head.

Six months: can sit up without support. For about a second and a half. Then rolls over, hits the floor and bursts into tears. Can hold its bottle or beaker, transfer small things from one hand to another, take telephone messages, vacuum the carpet.

This may not seem like particularly swift progress, and compared to most animals it isn't. By the time they are six months old many farm animals have already been eaten. But if you are watching your child develop from day to day, every small step he or she makes feels like a giant leap for mankind. Most days bring something new, even it's only a particular look on Junior's face when you are trying to change a nappy. Needless to say you become enthralled by all this and can't stop yourself telling everyone about it (see the section on Baby Bores in the next chapter). The system works well, for while the parents are congratulating themselves on every tiny new skill their baby acquires, Junior is actually concentrating on his or her core activities: eating, farting, pissing, shitting, vomiting, gurgling, wriggling, making silly noises, crying, sleeping, failing to sleep and (if you are lucky) looking adorable. Not to mention growing. Compare a four-month-old child with a newborn and they seem like different species. A twelve-month-old is incomprehensibly huge. Baby's priorities are clear: size first, skills later.

And how about you, six months down the line? How are you feeling? I believe it takes most fathers at least four months after the birth to remember that they are still alive. (It may take them longer to stop wishing they were dead, but that's another matter.)

Scarcely recognising the elderly heavy metal vocalist in the mirror in the morning, you may start to take stock of the situation. We must try not to generalise too much here: by six months babies are already demonstrating an extraordinary variety of behaviour patterns and personality traits. Some parents will now be past the worst, while others will still be knee deep in it, and finding it impossible to wash off in the shower every morning. What should be apparent, though, is that mentally and spiritually, Junior is now very much with us. Very tiny babies have a slightly unworldly quality – 'trailing clouds of glory', as Wordsworth put it. They are in the world, but not quite of it yet. Some cultures believe that their spirits join us only gradually, from wherever they were before. (Before fatherhood I couldn't have read that sentence without laughing, let alone written it. After two children, I can almost see what they mean.) But by six months the mind is fully engaged, and your baby is lying there just as you or I would be, wondering idly where the next meal is coming from. You, of course, have rather more to worry about.

SEX

Well, obviously there won't be any of that. The very thought. Go and stick it in a tree. Bloody hell, you're lucky still to be in the same bed.

In the weeks immediately after the birth, this won't matter. You will be far too tired to have sex with anyone, even yourself. Your beloved may have trouble sitting down. You wouldn't want her stitches to burst at the wrong moment. Before her memories fade (as biology dictates) your beloved will vividly remember how painful and humiliating the birth was and whose fault it was.

But three or four months later? If she had a bad delivery she may be still be sore. Also, breastfeeding can reduce a woman's libido. And much of the time she is exhausted and wants to be left alone. Unfortunately your ears are going purple and you are breathing so heavily your teeth are in danger of coming loose. You have three choices:

(a) Extra-marital affair. Though expensive and usually self-defeating, this is the option selected by many first-time fathers with purple ears. Unfortunately, the drink that dulls the guilt that enables them to do it in the first place also makes them liable to forget or fudge the issue of contraception. Result: more babies. You may love being a father, but probably not that much.

(b) Self-abuse. According to *New Scientist* magazine (which I must read more often) regular masturbators are 33 per cent less likely to fall prey to aggressive prostate cancer later in life. (Regular is defined here as five tugs a week or more.) 10,000 British men a year are killed by prostate cancer. So, lack of sex may not be the end of everything. Indeed, it may give you the chance to extend your life without sex by several decades.[26]

(c) Stick it in a tree. Brace and bit are available from all good hardware stores. Trees are available from all good forests. Have fun.

---

26. You may also be interested to learn that regular pizza eaters are 59 per cent less likely to catch cancer of the oesophagus. Statistics like this should be cherished, nurtured and stroked just in case they turn out to be true.

JEALOUSY

This may or may not be connected to the Sex problem. Less frivolously, it may cut to the very heart of your relationship with the mother of your child. Many men feel *fantastically* jealous of the relationship between mother and child – especially if the child is a boy. He has supplanted you in her affections. She loves him more than you. She wouldn't notice now if you dropped dead at her feet. All the above are true, but it's up to you how you respond to it.

Much depends on how good your relationship was before the baby came along. Men who have got used to being looked after by indulgent motherly women who are always cooking tend to come off worst here. Given a real baby, indulgent motherly women change their focus. The bloke is left to wonder where his next meal is coming from. She will let him back into her bed eventually, but only to make more babies. She doesn't even tell him off any more – not the way she used to.

Men who thought they had found their soulmate or *compadre* – well, they tend to come off worst as well. It may be that such men didn't particularly want children because they felt everything was as good as it could be. Their soulmate persuades them otherwise. So they go through pregnancy, birth, vomit and sleeplessness before realising that they were right all along. A tough call.

Easiest of all, is if you felt only mild affection for your partner, and couldn't give a monkeys whether or not she prefers her child to you. But you can't fake this. Indifference, like true love, has to be sincere. If you have to work at it, you've got no hope.

SQUALOR

There's something different about your flat/house,[27] isn't there? You've changed the curtains? New carpet? Different furniture? No, I know what it is. You've got all the same stuff as before, but now it's covered with sick.

Six months can be a lifetime for soft furnishings. Items that might have lasted decades if they only came into contact with adults, will be rubble after sustained abuse by babies. And this is before the baby can crawl and walk and knock things over, as it will in the months to come. People who are houseproud suffer the greatest agonies, as you would expect. You can keep Junior in nappies 23 hours and 56 minutes a day, and yet it will be in the other four minutes, when you have been momentarily distracted by a ringing phone, that your firstborn will squirt out a bowelful of steaming diarrhoea all over everything. And if you have a vomiter, there are no effective precautions you can take; you just have to hope. Carpets suffer the worst. Sofas are next in line. Curtains will be untouched if they are old and need replacing. New curtains will be spattered so artistically you may find yourself pretending it's part of the pattern.[28]

Amazingly, as with everything else, you seem to get used to it. When our son was just walking, he liked to get out of his nappy at every possible opportunity. Within a minute there would be a small puddle of urine somewhere. At first you mop

---

27. Delete as appropriate, or insert castle/shed/nifty warehouse conversion as you wish.

28. When midwives visit new mums, they become genuinely suspicious if the house is too clean. They know there aren't enough hours in the day to look after baby properly *and* do the bloody housework...

it up with 53 sheets of kitchen roll and pour on a bucketful of antiseptic. But there will come a time when *you won't bother to mop it up at all*. You can't be fucked. It's only a carpet. It'll survive. (Urine, you will argue, is sterile. What harm can it do? You and your partner will then try to remember which batty 1960s actress used to drink her own pee, by which time it will have soaked in anyway. Soon you may even argue that it strengthens the carpet weave.)

It won't just be you who descends so willingly into squalor. The mother of your child will accompany you all the way. She may even sprint on ahead. The more time you spend with your baby, the quicker your standards will fall. If your flat is as tiny as mine they don't so much fall as plummet. People with large houses and pots of money can try to localise the squalor, but most of us succumb in the end. Soon it's as much as we can do to take the mysterious pubic hairs out of our recently delivered pizza. Parenthood sets free the Wayne and Waynetta Slob within us all.

WEANING AND FEEDING

Between four and six months, most babies start to take solid food. You can usually tell when to phase it in: they become extremely hungry. Nutritionally, breast milk just ain't enough any more. (Psychologically, is another matter. Some babies go on guzzling at the breast until they are two years old. They just like being there. Who wouldn't?)

And so gloop comes into your life. You can buy ready-made gloop from supermarkets. You can make your own. In our flat babies always knew that breakfast or lunch was on its way by the sound of a whirring food processor down in the kitchen. My girlfriend, who has strong views about organic food, believes that shop-bought gloop is an instrument of the devil, for she has sadly missed her calling as a rabble-rousing demagogue. But wherever the gloop comes from, it's still gloop, because that's all babies can digest at this stage. And all gloop has one significant characteristic: it gets everywhere. No wall is safe from gloop. Few ceilings are immune. That isn't birdshit on your shoulder. And that isn't wax clogging up your ear.

Gloop falls into two categories: sweet gloop and savoury gloop. Baby will love sweet gloop. Mother will want to feed baby savoury gloop because she says it is better for baby. Baby will turn its nose up. Baby will refuse the spoon. Baby will cry. Mother will say, that's what I have prepared and that's all there is. Baby will cry some more. Mother will say you're not getting round me like that. Baby will turn up the volume. Grains of plaster will fall from the ceiling. Mother will say 'Fuck it' and latch baby onto her bosom in high dudgeon. Baby will guzzle loudly in celebration of its victory. Father will slope off to the kitchen and gloomily start mashing up a banana.

Because baby has a point. The first gloop it will encounter, which is usually just baby rice (a powdered substance of unknown provenance) and fruit pulp mashed up, does taste absolutely disgusting. Many of us have fond memories of those little Heinz baby food tins, some of which passed muster as pudding when you were as old as six or seven. (I remember one in particular called Apples, Prunes & Custard, which to my yobbish palate was close to sublime. In my imagination I can taste it now.) But these are for children who can process the added sugar and salt that makes grown-up food even vaguely palatable. Babies must eat more carefully. They must eat gloop.

And for a few meals, upon which a heavenly light shines, they will do just that. You put the spoon in the gloop, baby opens its mouth, you put the spoon in the mouth. Hey, this is easy, you think. But baby learns fast. A six-month-old can reach out for objects with its fingers, can bang the table and can shove finger foods into its mouth with moderate success. Baby looks at the spoon. Baby thinks, I can do that. Baby grabs the spoon from you. Gloop goes everywhere.

This is the first battle you will fight at mealtimes – the first of maybe 5,782. Baby will want to feed itself, will seek Power Over The Spoon. Baby will soon discover that a spoon can be bashed on the table, not just once but thousands of times, and that gloop can be splashed about in millions of amusing ways. After a while you run out of patience, give up on the meal – because nothing is being eaten – and go and do something else. Half an hour later baby will remember that it's hungry and start wailing again.

Later battles over food are not within the scope of this book, thank God, but if I ever write a sequel, they will get a whole chapter. Children's tastes in food are unpredictable and constantly mutating. Some children like everything; most don't. I must confess for the record that I was an outstandingly fussy eater as a child. I just didn't like most foods. Without peanut butter and baked beans (and the occasional tin of Apples, Prunes & Custard) I might well have starved. My father was convinced

I was doing this purely to annoy him, which shows how self-centred he was. We waged our Brussels Sprout Wars for 15 years before he admitted defeat and ran off with the au pair. I like lots of foods now. (But still not Brussels sprouts.)

WASHING MACHINE

This is your main weapon against squalor. You would never have guessed this, in the ease and luxury of your previous existence. The washing machine sat in a corner, occasionally washing things, as its warranty promised. Mine had lasted well over ten years, had never needed repairing, was only really used twice a week, in traditional bachelor fashion. One wash for whites, one wash for coloureds. Then a few years later, one wash for whites, one wash for coloureds, one wash for whites you'd mistakenly put in with the coloureds. Even when my girlfriend moved in, and the number of whites mistakenly put in with coloureds doubled, the machine kept going. And then the baby came along.

Call me oddball, but I believe washing machines make a different noise after a baby comes along. During their many wash, rinse and spin cycles they sound in pain, as though remembering the ease and luxury of their previous existence. Many pack up almost immediately: I don't think 'suicide' is too strong a word for this. Ours showed a self-destructive streak but could not bring itself to end it all. First the dial fell off, so you could only guess which program you were switching on. When we had sorted this out with Blu-tack, the machine sprang a leak. Apparently one of the pipes had spontaneously tied a knot in itself. A few weeks later the door fell off, but we stuck it back on and somehow (mainly involving a lot of string) managed to keep the damn thing going for another year or so. Then the second baby came along.

Now we have a new washing machine. It has digital displays and flashing red lights. It takes three loads a day without whining. You can even time it to switch on early in the morning, when you are standing right next to it, pouring the tea, with coated tongue and sulphurous breath after an evening out and four hours of interrupted sleep. It knows, I tell you. It knows.

CHINS

Between three and six months many babies start to compile an impressive collection of chins. Having come into the world with just the one, an averagely hungry infant will add a second, a third, maybe even a fourth. And these are only the ones on the surface. Delve between the accumulated chin masses and you will discover secret underchins, each of them storing lost droplets of milk that have long since gone off and turned into cheese. Unless scrupulously washed at least once a day, these dank zones can become the cause of what non-parents call 'baby smell' – that faintly sickly, dairy whiff that parents hope to become immune to but never will. It's the smell of ineptly dried laundry, with added curds and whey. See the proud parents handing over their baby to a close friend who instantly recoils as though lashed with a whip. Not every baby has a baby smell, but enough do to give them all a bad reputation. Nonetheless it can be overcome. It takes a brave man to probe the deepest recesses of his infant's chinzone with a moistened cotton bud. You are that man.

Note that a multitude of chins does not necessarily mean your baby is fat. Babies need to put on weight somewhere, and the vacant neck area is as good a place as any. Just because the baby looks fat doesn't mean that it is fat. All babies put on lots of weight, then suddenly grow an inch and look slim again. Their physical development comes in a series of lurches outwards and upwards: the weight they amass essentially fuels each increase in height. A genuinely obese baby is beyond plumpness; their arms and legs look like sausages that are about to burst. Babies like these are storing up a whole smorgasbord of health problems for later life, and are relatively unlikely to represent their country at any sport (other than darts). But don't be concerned by plumpness. A former model of my acquaintance only ever gave her baby daughter skimmed milk because she didn't want her to get fat. Tragically, though, this woman was an idiot. Feed your baby normally and healthily and you can't go wrong.

OUT AND ABOUT

Mother and baby begin as a package; slowly, painfully, they separate into two slightly surprised individuals. Eventually, with a stifled little sob, your partner will let you take Junior out for a stroll in either sling, pram or pushchair. So starts the next phase of fatherhood – you and your baby out and about, proud dad and sweet child, while your partner stays at home and puts her feet up. When baby is very small and sleeping a lot, you can go to the pub. I stood outside in the beer garden if I could, to avoid going home with a baby smelling of roll-ups and dead lager. Later on you can take Junior to parks and playgrounds to loiter with other sad dads or eye up the foxier mums. During the week there are usually more foxy mums than sad dads, which is nice. Faced with this numerical skew, many sad dads become surprisingly cheerful well-groomed dads with a twinkle in their eye. Some may not be dads at all, but unscrupulous single friends of dads who are renting Junior by the hour. Having a small child attached to you makes it so much easier to spark up conversations in parks and playgrounds, as you will find out for yourself.

Indeed, these trips out can be wonderful balm for the battered paternal ego, especially if your child is a looker. Beautiful babies mean good, strong genes, and are the most effective advertisement yet devised for the contents of your trousers. As a result, some women passing you on the street will give you the most amazing looks. They never looked at you like that when you were single. It will make you think and wonder, and may confirm your suspicion that some women are only after one thing. Good grief! If only you had known then what you know now! You would have ten children, be three times divorced and drinking solvent from a brown paper bag. Sometimes it's better to know nothing at all.

YOUR BODY: AN UPDATE

- Shoulders and upper arms: strengthened, especially on the side you most frequently carry Junior.
- Thighs and calves: rock hard after hours of jogging and dancing Junior to sleep.
- Feet: sore and blistered after ditto.
- Lower back: catastrophically fucked.
- Stomach muscles: gone to rack and ruin. Excessive pizza intake hasn't helped.
- Skin: grey, with red blotches.
- Bowels: don't ask.
- Hair: emigrating from head to ears and nose.
- Pubes: going grey.
- Internal organs: withered.
- External organ: semi-retired.
- Prospects: more of the same.

BATHTIME

This, by strange tradition, is a father's job. Dad gets home from work, carrying briefcase (empty) and mopping brow, and immediately goes into bathroom where photogenic children are already frolicking in mounds of bubbles. We have seen it a thousand times on TV, and now many of us are doing it for ourselves. I suppose it makes sense: if their mother has been with them all day, she wants nothing more at this stage than to climb into a large glass of white wine. She does not want to wash faces, brush teeth or rescue plastic ducks that have fallen out of the bath for the thirty-eighth time in ten minutes. But even if mother hasn't been with them all day, or father has, it's still father who does the bath. Maybe it's because Entertainer Dad has the knack of transforming a tiresome chore into something more fun. Or maybe he has just been outmanoeuvred. No one knows for sure.

So it is you who sits on the loo reading old newspapers while your child pours you endless cups of 'tea' out of an old plastic teapot. Somehow it is taken for granted that every child needs a bath every day, although you never did at that age and neither did anyone else. (What is different is that our parents scrubbed us from head to toe with viciously medicated soap that stripped away the top three layers of our skin. Now you are recommended not to use soap at all for the first few months, and sparingly thereafter. This makes much more sense. Children don't actually need to be that clean. Children who grow up on farms famously have stronger immune systems than anybody.)

When your baby is five or six months old it may well discover its genitals. If you think about it, the bath is the perfect place to do this. The rest of the time Junior is encased in nappies. Also, in most cases, there is a big fat stomach in the way, as there will be for you soon, if there isn't already. In soothing warm water the fingers can explore hidden regions more effectively. Before you know it, your innocent little baby, who cannot walk or talk yet, will be tugging away like a teenager. Maybe I am unusually shockable, but I was taken aback by this, as by the beatific expression of ecstasy that accompanied it. But it's normal behaviour. All they know is that it feels nice, and we cannot argue with that. Their tugging has nothing to do with sex, and everything to do with the process of discovering what their body can do, before inhibitions arrive and make them forget again. Don't draw attention to it; just let them get on with it. In the meantime you start to wonder: how did your parents react when you did it? Ten points and a gold star if you have the gumption to ask them.

Incidentally, beware of plastic bath toys. As with soft toys, other people buy them, then they start to breed. The difference is that after a few years soft toys fall apart. Plastic bath toys are here for good. Centuries hence, when mankind has bickered itself into extinction, small grinning yellow non-biodegradable ducks will rule the world. It's only a hunch, but I think they might do it quite well.

GO BACK TO WORK

It hardly seems fair, but one of you had to. I'm sure you almost sobbed at the door as you left home on your first day back, and certainly did not skip or gambol down the road like a newborn lamb. Six months on, many mothers are thinking of returning to work as well. Indeed, some will already have gone back, having handed over daily care of baba to a grandparent, a registered childminder, a Bosnian au pair with bad skin and an ankle bracelet, or the prestigious and expensive Dotheboys Nursery in the next street but one. Their sense of relief will have been compounded by the absolute certainty that their baby is getting the best possible care, learning social skills sooner than most babies and almost painfully happy to see mummy and daddy in the evening, if they can tear themselves away from the office soon enough. Which, to me at least, begs an important question: if you are going to do this to them, why have the fucking babies in the first place?

This is a complicated and emotive issue, about which everyone has fierce opinions. For what it's worth, I do not believe that Woman's Place Is In The Home. It would be nice (although naive) to be able to say that things have moved on a little since anyone genuinely thought this. If a mother prefers her old job to the grind of parenthood, who can blame her? I certainly prefer writing this book to reading *The Gruffalo* to my children for the six-hundredth time. There is also the question of money. In our materialistic and debt-crazed society, many couples need two incomes to avoid penury. And whatever your circumstances, if you can find someone else to look after the baby who gives it all the love and care and attention it needs, and you can afford it, then great. I know a working single mother who shares care of her daughter very successfully with her own mother. And I know middle-class parents who have found wonderful, loving, dedicated nannies who have stuck around for years and given the children everything they needed.

But.

The main priority – the only priority – has to be the needs of the baby. And until they are two years old, what they need more than anything is a mother or a father. It doesn't matter which. If you disregard breastfeeding, there is no identifiable difference between a father's full-time care and a mother's full-time care.

A baby will thrive with either parent as long as that parent looks after the baby properly. And the same applies to a designated carer who loves the baby as much, or nearly as much, as you do.

What a six-month-old baby does not need– and this is just my opinion, so disregard it if you wish – is to be dumped in a nursery with a lot of other babies for eight hours a day, five days a week. They don't need their social skills sharpened; they need love, and they need one-to-one attention. Even with the best of all possible intentions, nursery staff cannot give them these things. By the age of two most babies are ready for a little socialising, but full-time nursery before the age of one is a stark choice for a little baby. Put it this way: there is no way I could do it.

One solution, of course, is that you could become a house-husband. Send the missis back to work, settle down for the day with the remote control ... and then give her a hard time when she rolls in late from work smelling faintly of white wine spritzers.

> *ANTHONY: I go to playgroups and so on and mums hardly ever look at you, let alone talk to you. You can see them huddling around their kids protecting them against this abuser in their midst! The toy library was brilliant for easing me through this. The staff there were really glad to have a man around and really encouraged the other mums to interact with me. But there are moments of hurt. When R was three months old, Astrid went to Spain on a job; so I looked after him for three weeks on my own. The day after she got back we went to a party. All the women there immediately talked to Astrid about R. I wanted to tell them how he was eating, wanted to have a row about MMR, wanted to talk*

babies basically and no one would enter into a conversation with me. Presumably the assumption was that I knew nothing. Or wasn't interested. The joke was I felt so isolated I spent the party in the front room with all the kids, playing with them. Then, when the party was over, the mums trolled in and rounded up their kids. No one seemed to notice I was there, looking after them. Heigh ho. Ah, poor dads.

21 competitive dad, baby bore

No, no, no – you're thinking at this moment – that's not me. Competitive Dad ... Baby Bore ... no, no, not me.

Are you sure?

A couple of years ago, when I was first thinking about writing this book, I was sitting at my desk one morning, staring out of the window, and vaguely wondering whether I should go down to the kitchen and get a biscuit. (The writer's life in a nutshell.) Then I spotted a man pushing a pushchair on the other side of the street. The expression on his face was beatific. He was a proud father and no mistake. I was impressed. How refreshing in these cynical times that a man should feel so enriched by the mere fact of fatherhood. He was a turkey cock of new fathers, displaying his progeny with swollen chest and ruffled feathers. I hadn't seen anyone look so thoroughly pleased with himself in years.

And then I worked it out. The child in the pushchair was turning his head and shouting, 'Daddy! Daddy!' and Daddy wasn't paying the slightest bit of attention. Daddy wasn't proud of his child. Daddy was proud of his child's pushchair. It was one of the first three-wheeler models, big and nasty and expensive, a hot rod of pushchairs, and a precursor of what we now know as ATPs (all-terrain pushchairs). It had clearly cost him a fortune, and he may have been wondering whether to have go-faster stripes stuck on. He was a man with a vehicle. He wanted other men to see him and admire him, he wanted women to fall over him. Who needs a Porsche, when you are piloting the Rolls-Royce of pushchairs?

There is something of this man, this sad, sorry tosser, in all of us. He had no real need of an all-terrain pushchair, as he was not planning to propel his toddler across wasteland or open countryside. He lived in suburbia, and rarely walked further than the newsagents. And yet his drive to compete had found a new and unexpected outlet. He knew he was one of the first people to buy one of these things, and that other people would see it and want one too. When I say 'other people' I naturally mean other men. When you see a woman with heavy shopping irritably pushing an ATP along a high street, you can bet your trousers that a man bought it for her. Most mothers prefer foldaway buggies, which are smaller and far more practical, but useless on swamp and tundra. How stubbornly unromantic women are, how limited their horizons.

Where women who have had children gather together, the talk is usually about children. Where men who have had children gather together, the talk is usually about football or work or films you haven't seen or, if at a boring family event, the route you took to get here. You didn't turn left after the bypass? Well, you'll know better for next time. Just occasionally, though, if you are with men you know very well, and you are feeling suitably relaxed and the drink is flowing and all nine planets are in alignment, you might venture to discuss something closer to your heart: such as which model of baby monitor to buy. 'What, you've only got the TX2000? We just picked up the 3000 the other day. 28 per cent greater range, graphic equaliser, hi-fi voice reproduction, rechargeable batteries. Virtually impossible to find in the shops, of course, but I know a good website which should be able to do it. Although you'd probably need a credit card with a US billing address ... '

Mothers compete as well, of course, but only over the children. If one pre-school child has started biting or scratching, the mothers of all the other pre-school children will discuss it with a combination of stern disapproval and unabashed glee. But their competitive instincts tend to be reactive. In other words they actually need something to be competitive about. We don't. Example: if you told me I had an ugly baby, I would be grievously offended. But if you told me that you had an ugly baby, I would probably say that mine was uglier. Competitive Dad is competitive first, and dad about fourth. He knows that his first baby was 9lb 2oz at birth, because someone else he knew had one that was 9lb 1oz. That single ounce may not make much difference now, but who knows? Half a century down the line it may make the difference between Nobel prize and no Nobel prize. With the latter remaining odds-on favourite, obviously.

Women find all this a bit sad. It probably is, but it is also standard bloke behaviour. If we are all like this – and on some level, I believe we are – then we as individuals cannot be blamed for being like this, which gives us permission to go on being like this forever. All Competitive Dad ever needs is an audience:

> Russell Crowe turned into the Dadiator after splashing out £50,000 on a cot for his son.
>
> The *Gladiator* star spent over £150,000 on stuff for his boy Charles's nursery.
>
> Russell has told friends: 'I want nothing but the best for my boy – whatever the cost. He's going to have the best and coolest nursery in Australia.'
>
> The cot is a 19th-century Scandinavian design with ornate carvings. Also on his shopping list were some bedside lamps, and a painting called 'Reflection Of A Boy' – worth £75,000 – for the nursery wall.
>
> A source said: 'Russell chose all the items himself. It's clear he has got a really good eye.'

I know men who have set sweepstakes for their baby's birth weight. I know men who, having set sweepstakes for their baby's birth weight, have then spread-bet substantial sums on same. Who needs sport when you have the tidal wave of statistics childbirth can throw up? If you are determined enough you can bet on almost anything:

- proximity of birth to due date;
- weight of baby at birth;
- weight of baby after 28 days given weight of baby at birth;
- date of first crawling, date of first word spoken, date of first walking (as corroborated by independent witness, i.e. your partner);
- your own life expectancy should your partner find out about any of this.

As men, happily, we have the gift of compartmentalising different parts of our lives and, indeed, our personalities, so that none of them ever have to meet. In this box over here is Nurturing Dad, who is warm and loving. In the box next door is our old friend from the Equal Opportunities Commission report, Enforcer Dad, and in other boxes are his mates, Entertainer Dad and Useful Dad. And then in the furthest box, just beyond normal vision, is the one no one acknowledges, the one that dare not speak his name: Competitive Dad. We are the sum of our compartments, but each compartment is independent and may rarely have contact with any of the others. What would Nurturing Dad and Competitive Dad talk about? Nurturing Dad loves taking photographs of his baby; Competitive Dad only wants to know what camera he has got. If they met at a party they would stand there holding their glasses of wine for a few seconds and then wander off to talk to someone else. Maybe some of your 83 other sub-personalities – including Eight-Year-Old Boy, Sulky Masturbating Teenager and Disgraced Pensioner – could bring them together, but somehow I doubt it.

It is Nurturing Dad who picks up that big hardback parenthood manual, the one with all the colour pictures of men with beards massaging pregnant women with foul smelling oils, and reads it seriously, hoping to pick up tips. It is Useful Dad who bought the book in the first place (for his partner, not for himself), and it is Entertainer Dad who will help his small child cut it into tiny pieces in about three years' time. Competitive Dad flicks through the pages, idly looking for photos of breasts, until he finds a really good table, or possibly a chart, and then he gets interested. Is his baby advanced for his age? If average babies walk at around a year, Competitive Dad will want to tell his friends that his baby spontaneously broke into a sprint at eight and a half months. It varies. I have a Competitive Dad friend who rings up mainly to tell me how clever his children are. As I tend to stop listening, I can't give you many details, but I do have a mental picture of them in their local library, the four-year-old translating Socratic dialogues for fun while the older boy moves the books from shelf to shelf because he has thought up something more efficient and elegant than the Dewey decimal system.

But who am I to talk? This morning I took my boy up to the main road so he could do his favourite thing of the moment, viz. point at lorries and diggers and cars and shout 'Lorry!' or 'Digger!' or 'Car!' as appropriate. Then suddenly he shouted

'Grandma's car!' Speeding past was the same make and model of car as the one my mum has, but in a different colour. I hadn't recognised it, but he had, and he isn't even two. As I write this story down an hour or so later, it now seems amazingly pathetic, but the four people I told in the meantime all responded brightly and indulgently, as though this was a genuinely impressive achievement. And the half dozen or more people I will tell in the pub this evening may react similarly, before racing off to take urgent phone calls.

This is the flipside of Competitive Dad. This is Baby Bore. The two of them live in neighbouring compartments, and if both are allowed to escape at the same time you really are in trouble. Baby Bore lies dormant immediately after the birth, when you spend all your time and energy simply trying to cope, but once you have settled into the rhythms of fatherhood he bursts out of his box, ready to bore. Every tiny advance made by Junior is fuel for his anecdotes. The light shines from his eyes as he describes the latest achievement in forensic detail. Because he has never seen it before he cannot believe it is all so interesting. More damagingly, he cannot believe that everyone else doesn't find it interesting, too.

Let us not try to dampen Baby Bore's ardour. Watching your baby develop from day to day, work things out and add to the repertoire – these are some of the best things about being a father. What you may not have expected is how enthralling it is. One day Junior can grasp a spoon, and you think this is the most fascinating thing you have ever seen. Objectivity flies out of the window. This takes some men by surprise, especially those men accustomed to being rational and practical and not hopelessly sentimental bags of mush. But it is not mothers who sit in pubs telling their friends at unforgivable length that their four-month-old daughter smiled at herself in the mirror today. Brainwashed by love, we become the Moonies of parenthood. We tell everyone how great it is, and that they should do it. As we were never much good at listening in the first place, we don't notice that they are not listening and don't care. But still we drone on, glowing with pride and self-satisfaction, enjoying the story every bit as much as the first time we told it.

Women don't do this. The two sexes converse differently. Women smile more at the person they are talking to. They are more likely to pause and wait for a sign of agreement before continuing. Whereas men just stare into the middle distance and start talking. Women's bizarre and selfless willingness to listen to other people saves them from Baby Bore-hood; also the fact that they spend a lot of time in the company of people (i.e. women) who are also interested in babies. We spend our time with people (i.e. men) who are not interested in babies, and very specifically not interested in your baby. It's hard to know who comes off worst in these circumstances: the Baby Bore or the Baby Bored.

Happily, Baby Bore is more easily controlled than Competitive Dad. It is mainly a matter of selecting your audience. The following make bad audiences:

- People who have not had children. This includes single people (male or female), couples who don't want children, couples who can't have children, couples who are trying like mad to have children and so are permanently bad-tempered and exhausted, and couples who are putting off the question of whether to have children because they hate each other's guts but do not yet have the gumption to split up. Most of these people are delighted for you in your happiness. They will undertake to see a maximum of two photographs of your baby in any one calendar year. They may even buy Junior expensive and useful presents for birthdays and Christmas. But they do not want to know whether baby pushed out a rock-hard stool this morning or a chocolate mousse-style squisher. The friends who are fondest of you will suffer most in this regard: out of misplaced loyalty, they are the ones who won't leave the building whenever you start talking.

- People who have already had children. Maybe their kids are older, and one or two may already be pleading their innocence in Vietnamese jails, but whatever is going on in their stressful child-packed lives, your newly minted enthusiasm won't make them any happier. They know all about this stage (whatever stage it is) and they don't need to be reminded. And they will be less forgiving than the people who do not have children. Indeed, if provoked with too many stories of Junior's ribtickling escapades, they can turn nasty. It's a terrible thing to see valued old friends flipping instantaneously into implacable enemies, spiritually baring their fangs. Don't say you weren't warned.

The following make good audiences:

- The bathroom mirror. As pleased to see you as it ever was.

- Your partner. (Unless she is depressed and locked in her room crying, or the two of you are only communicating through solicitors, in which case it's back to the mirror.)

- Grandparents. The only people in the world who are even 50 per cent as interested in your baby as you and your partner are. Grandmothers like stories about how adorable your baby is, while grandfathers usually prefer empirical evidence of superior physical prowess. (For every Competitive Dad, there may be up to two Competitive Granddads.)

- Other people who had babies at around the same time as you. The window for this is surprisingly narrow. Anyone with a baby four months older or four months younger might as well be on a different planet. Ideal are people whose baby is virtually the same age but much uglier than yours. By a remarkable coincidence, this is probably the same way they see you.

It should come as no surprise, then, if your social circle shrinks a little in the months following the birth. My friend Russell, who is wilfully childless, sent me this Venn diagram when our first baby was born:

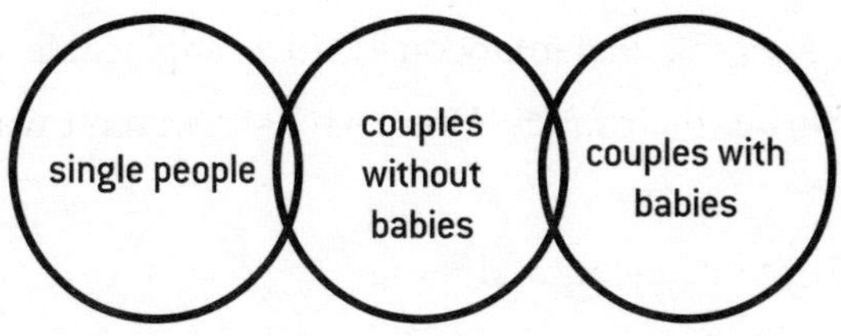

He wasn't trying to be unpleasant; it just represented his very particular strain of pessimism. After years of knocking about together, he knew we would not be knocking about together in the same way. And he was right, although we remain good friends. We have different lives now: his, much the same as it ever was, and mine, which involves going to bed roughly four hours before he does every night, and usually only to sleep. Friendships that can overcome the Venn diagram are worth fostering. Competitive Dad and Baby Bore threaten all friendships, and nearly all dealings with the outside world. Back in your box now, both of you. Lock it tight. And goodnight.

22
vinegar & brown paper

'When I was a child, I spake as a child, I understood as a child, I thought as a child; but when I became a man I put away childish things.' 1 Corinthians 13:1

They could be the deepest, darkest, most skilfully buried childhood memories of all ...

Baa baa black sheep, have you any wool? Yes sir, yes sir, three bags full. One for the master, one for the dame, and one for the little boy who lives down the lane.

Twinkle twinkle little star, how I wonder what you are[29]*. Up above the world so high, like a diamond in the sky, twinkle twinkle little star, how I wonder what you are*[30]*.*

Rock-a-bye baby on the tree top[31]*. When the wind blows the cradle will rock*[32]*. When the bough breaks the cradle will fall, and down will come baby, cradle and all*[33]*.*

---

29. You are a star, obviously.
30. I've told you already. You are a star.
31. And what is it doing there?
32. As you would expect.
33. Call Social Services!

Three blind mice, three blind mice, see how they run, see how they run[34]*. They all ran away from the farmer's wife, who cut off their tails with a carving knife. Did you ever see such a thing in your life as three blind mice?*

Well, no, is the simple answer to that. Poor mice. It's not even as though they were partially sighted. Now they are tailless as well as blind, with nasty suppurating wounds that require immediate medical attention. Meanwhile the farmer's wife chuckles evilly to herself. Who needs a cat?

You will ask yourself these questions and many others when you start singing your little one to sleep. Most nursery rhymes are either inane or fantastically violent. Many are both. Things you wouldn't want to see on TV, let alone in real life, are standard behaviour in the moral vacuum of nursery rhymes. And yet these are the sweet little tunes your baby will want hear again and again. I figure I have sung Rock-A-Bye Baby 3,000 times in the past five years, and Twinkle Twinkle Little Star more than 2,500 times. I know this because I was working it out in my head last night while singing Rock-A-Bye for the ninth or tenth time as the small boy finally drifted off. Add 1,500 Baa Baa Black Sheeps, 750 The Wheels On The Bus Go Round And Rounds and uncountable, edging-in-the-direction-of-infinite verses to Old Macdonald Had A Farm and you can see how music, like everything else, is changed irrevocably by parenthood. I have been writing about pop music for 15 years on and off and I still buy scarcely justifi-

34. A century of unspeakable laboratory experiments was inspired by this rhyme.

able quantities of new CDs. And yet, as I walked up the road to the sweet shop this morning, what was I whistling? Could it be the theme tune to Rosie And Jim, a forgotten kids' TV show of the 1990s? 'Rosie and Jim, Rosie and Jim ...' are sadly the only lyrics I know, for this is the featured melody on a tatty plastic musical box our daughter was given when she was six months old. Both our children have since played it to death, and the tune is now hard-wired into my brain. Sometimes I wake up in the night humming it. It's not only the words to nursery rhymes that are evil; the tunes are as well, which is why many of them have survived for hundreds of years.

There is a term, meme, to describe anything, a tune, a phrase, that sticks in your head whether you want it to or not. We are all susceptible to memes. Paul McCartney has composed a few. Advertising copywriters try to write little else. Nursery rhymes are all memes. The TV series The Fast Show was built around catchphrases, which are comedy's memes. Children tune into memes instinctively. Adults distrust them equally instinctively but have little effective defence against them. How can we expect otherwise? Getting into your head and staying there forever is what memes are for. If we can resist them they aren't memes. Nonetheless, a child's love of memes presents its parents with a challenge. Do you embrace, or reject? Join in, or keep your distance and your dignity? Your response to these questions could determine the whole tone of your parenthood.

Myself, I had never sung anywhere more public than a shower before. I have never contemplated entering 'Stars In Their Eyes' and impersonating Jarvis Cocker or Freddie Mercury for the lipsmacking amusement of millions. But as the father of small children, I have found myself singing the following words under a variety of embarrassing circumstances:

Jelly on a plate. Jelly on a plate. Wibble wobble wibble wobble, jelly on a plate.

(In case you don't know it, I should add that it has a neat little tune, and not a bad second verse:

Biscuits in the tin. Biscuits in the tin. Shake 'em up, shake 'em up, biscuits in the tin.)

You will do anything – literally anything – to amuse and distract a baby that is throwing a vast theatrical tantrum when you need it to be quiet. When you are changing a nappy, especially on a slightly undersized table in a department store loo. Or pushing the pushchair when you were supposed to be somewhere else ten minutes ago. On public transport. Especially on public transport. If singing 'Jelly On A Plate' will do it, that's what you will do. And you never know: with a bit of luck another passenger might strike up a harmony.

Row row row your boat, gently down the stream. Merrily merrily merrily merrily, life is but a dream. Row row row your boat, gently down the stream. If you see a crocodile, don't forget to scream.

(You emit a tiny strangled scream and the baby laughs.)

Soon you know not just all the nursery rhymes, but their alternative versions as well. For 'Row Row Row Your Boat', for which you row your infant backwards and forwards, there is an optional second verse starting 'Rock rock rock your boat ...', for which you rock your infant from side to side. Then there is the rarely used last verse variant, which goes:

Row row row your boat gently to the shore. If you see a lion there, don't forget to roar.

(You emit a tiny strangled roar and the baby laughs. When it can speak it will say 'More' and you will have to do it again and again and again for hours.)

A few old nursery rhymes incorporate jokes that only adults will understand. That's because they are not jokes as such, but archaisms whose meanings have changed over the centuries and have now become unintentionally funny. For instance:

Jack and Jill went up the hill to fetch a pail of water. Jack fell down and broke his crown and Jill came tumbling after.

This much we know. Crown, as you will explain to your toddler in a couple of years' time, is an old word for head and not the heavy bejewelled thing kings and queens wear. It is in verse two that the trouble starts. This is the original unbowdlerised version:

Then up Jack got, and home did trot, as fast as he could caper, to old Dame Dob, who patched his nob with vinegar and brown paper.

However many times I sing this, it still makes me laugh. I don't think I found it that funny before fatherhood.

The more you hang around small children, the more like them you become. Childishness turns out to be catching. With luck you will grow out of it, but probably not before your children do. You can either accept this, or you can have a big sulk about it, and go to your room without any dinner.

If you don't believe me, consider for a moment the area of your body south of your nipples and due north of your pubes. In our previous lives as adults we called this our stomach, or if we drank beer, our belly, or if we were doctors or fitness fanatics, our abdomens. Now it's our tummy. Kingsley Amis called this word 'insufferably arch' but then he wasn't a parent in the first decade of the new millennium. It is indeed a horrible mimsy cutesy word, and we all use it.

Now consider bodily functions. In this book, for comic effect, I have generally used words like shit and piss and vomit, as I did before I became a parent. Notwithstanding that most parents swear less anyway, because they don't want their child's first word to be 'cocksucker', you will veer away from shit and piss in normal conversation, towards poo and wee. 'Have you done a poo then?' you say to the baby as you prepare to change another nappy. The answer of course is 'Yes, you twat,' although happily the baby can't say that yet. The baby could add, 'Why are you talking in that ridiculous tone of voice?' because however hard you try not to, you do speak in a particular way to your infant. This baby voice is slightly higher pitched than normal, slightly slower and more clearly enunciated, and slightly more patronising. This is the way you might talk to a dog, or elderly upper-class people on holiday talk to waiters.

Words themselves begin to mutate. Some acquire inexplicable echoes. 'Eat your pud-pud.' 'Let's change your nap-nap. Ah, it's a poo-poo.' Extra vowels attach themselves. 'Come on, let's put on your vestie.' The other day I tried to tempt my son with the promise of a 'bathie'. Is this really supposed to sound more appealing than a dull old bath? One father I spoke to admitted that in his house 'pants' have become 'panters', which must be a bit worrying.

> *BASIL: Out walking, with or without the children, I now say 'I'm going to do wee-wee bush' rather than 'I'm going for a pee in those bushes.' My wife thinks I'm lucky not to have been arrested.*

Then there is the swaying to the music. Every parent does this when comforting their child. Only this time you are not comforting your child, there is no music and you are standing at the checkout in the supermarket paying for the weekly shop. Everyone is looking at you the way they look at loonies. You would look at you as if you were a loony, too, if you could.

Mothers who stay at home to look after their children start to wonder whether their minds are going. 'Oh for some adult company!' sighs my girlfriend from time to time, giving me the sort of look that makes it clear I don't count. Women who used to work full time, especially in high-powered jobs, become convinced that the loss of these jobs turns them into morons. What they never notice is that the men in their lives, the ones going out to work every day as usual, are also turning into morons. It's babies wot do it. You go to the playground for the first time and you look around at all these wonderful contraptions they now have, the huge climbing frames and rope bridges and long slides and sandpits, and what do you think? Do you think, 'Wow! My baby is going to love playing in this when he/she is a bit older?'

No, you don't. You think, 'They never had playgrounds like this when I was little.'

Then you go to the toy shop, ostensibly to buy something for your infant, or maybe to avoid real shopping. You try and look around the shelves with a baby's eye. Would Junior like this? Is that too old or too young or too expensive? This lasts twelve seconds, for that's how long it takes you to find something you want to buy for yourself. For me, it was one of those ruinously expensive Brio wooden railway sets, which I bought for my daughter before she could walk. After you get the basics there are some terrific accessories to collect: junctions, bridges, stations, level crossings. Eventually your child will be old enough to play with it, but you will probably have moved onto something else by then.

(As with so much in this book I thought I was the only person who did this, until I started asking around. Several dads told me of the cheap pseudo-Brio tracks you can buy at Tesco. One showed me a great little three-point junction he had picked up somewhere on a business trip.)

'When I became a man I put away childish things.' Now we are buying childish things again, and playing with them. Fathers used to be distant, slightly scary figures who had fought wars. Even today, some dads feel the need to be jaw-droppingly pompous, although I think we can recognise this as a lack of confidence as much as anything else. Join in, or keep your distance and your dignity? It's not that hard a choice. Better, I believe, to acknowledge that the infantilisation of parents is a natural process. You can only play with your child if you know how to play at all, and if you have forgotten you can learn again. It is funny that we spend all those years in our teens and twenties trying to be cool, learning to put an adult face on, to be men who maybe don't smile much and certainly try and show no weakness if we can possibly help it. Work culture punishes weakness mercilessly; most male peer groups do. Babies render this invalid. You cannot be cool or authoritative or scary with a blob of baby puke on your tie. Hey, and there's Lego and roller-coasters to come. This is the true maturity, I believe: the realisation that all your formerly held notions of maturity were completely immature. Go on, have some more pud-pud. Jelly on a plate, jelly on a plate, wibble wobble wibble wobble, jelly on a plate ...

23
mr bad example

And so for your final station stop on this Vermilion Books service, the first birthday party. Change here for Terrible Twos, Potty Training, Playgroup, Sibling Rivalry, Primary School, Pester Power and all stations to Adolescence. Please could passengers remember to take all their belongings with them, including the baby bath I suggested they get and which they now can't get rid of. On behalf of Vermilion Books I would like to thank you for travelling with us today, and we hope to see you again soon. First birthday party. We are now approaching first birthday party.

It has been a long haul. Most passengers preparing to disembark have aged visibly since the start of the journey, and all could do with a good night's sleep. A few will be heading straight for the station bar. And yet it is only 21 months since your baby was conceived, since that tiny sperm with your face crash-landed into your partner's huge angry egg. In the grand sweep of a human lifespan, this is no time at all. But to you, as you plant a single candle in the centre of your firstborn's cake, it feels like the best part of a decade.

Junior should now be crawling, if not walking. Parents can be in a hurry for their progeny to get stomping, but those couple of months on all fours should not be underestimated: they represent a significant stage in Junior's development. Babies cheer up enormously when they start to move. They will try standing up, and may do some nonchalant leaning against chairs, before falling over with the usual clunk. But it is crawling rather than walking that opens the world up to them. They will expend vast efforts trying to crawl. At first they will be able to crawl backwards. This is progress, although they don't usually want to go that way at all. Imagine that the toy you want is almost within reach, so you try and crawl towards it and end up further away than when you started. Admittedly, most of the rest of life is like this, but it's a hard lesson to learn when you aren't even a year old.

Crawling, though, means power over your own destiny. For the first time in your short life as a baby, you can go where you want. I am writing this sitting in a park. Not far from me a conspicuously foxy young mother has put her infant down on the grass while she talks on her mobile. Infant crawls towards another woman nearby. Foxy young mother doesn't want infant to bother the other woman, so she picks her up and puts her down a little way away, facing the opposite direction. Infant immediately turns round and heads back to the other woman. Foxy young mother gives up and carries on chatting on her phone. Infant and the other woman make friends. Infant has won. She gurgles with pleasure.

Walking impresses adults more, but to baby, I suspect, it's merely the next stage. (Baby is actually thinking about running when it starts walking. When it learns to run, it will be more concerned with jumping.) At twelve months some babies will be walking, although not all. Boys tend to walk before girls, and younger siblings earlier than firstborns.

Crawling and walking change everything, as you would imagine. From now on you must always strap in Junior to the pushchair to prevent untimely escape attempts (such as when you are halfway across a pedestrian crossing or near the front of a long queue in the Post Office). Indoors, you will be thinking about putting all breakables out of reach. This is easily managed when baby is crawling, a little more challenging when baby is walking, and completely impossible when baby learns to jump and climb all over the place like a gibbon. With a three-year-old in the house, *everything* is breakable. Or, at the very least, spillable. (The most expensive toys in the world can never be as interesting to a young mind as a big bag of uncooked rice that can be poured all over the kitchen floor.) Thus begin the Tidying Up Years. Valuable heirlooms, if fragile, are better off sold or kept in a safe or, possibly better still, stolen and claimed on the insurance. Parents of small children find it amazingly easy to fake burglaries, as their house tends to look like that all the time anyway.

PC no. 456: 'Oh, God they've smeared shit on the walls.'

Tearful householder: 'What sort of people would do such a thing?'

At a year old Junior is unlikely to talk, beyond the odd word like 'dog' or 'catamaran'. (So will be unlikely to give you away to the police in the scenario above.) But he or she can follow conversations and make the odd sound to fill the gaps. You can read simple stories to your baby, let it play with non-toxic crayons which it will eat, and encourage it to stand unaided for a second or two. Soon this baby will be a baby no longer, but a *toddler*. You won't be ready for that, either.

For the pressure does not let up. Once or twice in this book I have used phrases like 'being past the worst' which may have been interpreted by a few, sad, literal-minded readers as implying that everything calms down after a while. What I should have written, to maintain absolute accuracy, was 'being past *a* worst', because you are barely past one particular worst before two or three more start bearing down on you. Only Enforcer Dad, Absentee Dad and rarer beasts like Bigamist Dad seem to escape this process. The rest of us, mothers and fathers alike, must accept our fate. You start dreaming of alternative lives you might have led. You wonder what would have happened if you had had babies with that woman, instead of this woman. (Exactly the same, I guarantee.) You imagine yourself travelling light, with just a passport and an old rucksack, having wild new adventures every day, not missing home a bit. You remember happy nights in the boozer with all your other miserable single friends. You envy young people and the witless, doomed way they seem to drift through life.

Women think such things, too, or their womanly equivalents. But they are better at hiding it. That is to say, they are better at pretending that they have never even imagined that anyone could think such things, and that anyone who does is reprehensible to the point of criminality. The Tiredness Olympics were just one event. These days you are competing in a full decathlon.

Children change a relationship. How can they not? In the early stages of your relationship, your beloved's responses to you broke down roughly as follows:

- Love 14%.
- Amused tolerance 17%.
- Thinking of having your babies 23%.
- Looking forward to changing your hairstyle, clothes, furniture etc. 38%.
- Faint concern at the back of her mind that she can do better 8%.

And after a year of parenthood:

- Sighs of disappointment 31%.
- Raging certainty that she could have done better 43%.
- Wondering what on earth she was thinking of 15%.
- Contemplating adultery/divorce/murder 11%.

And this is without you having done anything to provoke her. Or anything at all really.

Contradiction, though, lies at the heart of parenthood. So does unpredictability. One day, and this could happen any time after Junior's first birthday, she will start smiling at you again. Weirder still, flirting with you again. She will say complimentary things to you when you are least expecting it (such as when you are awake). She will make faint suggestions during commercial breaks that she might respond favourably to your sexual advances. She will poke tiny holes in all your condoms. She will want your sperm again, and when you are drunk she will probably have it.

For as Junior learns to crawl and begins literally to move beyond babyhood, your beloved will feel a yearning for another one. Her amnesia is complete, her glasses are tinted with rose. You can show her slides of the first birth, or selected video highlights; nothing will budge her. This time will be different, she will say. And besides, little Arbuthnot/Iolanthe needs a playmate. Much as you will *need* to find the money to buy somewhere bigger to live, a larger car and oodles more stuff to keep the family in the style to which it has become accustomed before you peg out with a coronary in 15 years' time.

Don't blame her. It is her body talking. Just as your male body tells you to impregnate as many women as you can, her female body tells her to make the most of your male body before you peg out with a coronary in 15 years' time.

And in the essentials she is right. The second birth usually is easier than the first. The female body is designed to give birth to lots of children. The first one is effectively a trial run. By the fourth or fifth they almost drop out of their own accord.

And while Arbuthnot or Iolanthe does not need a playmate as such, or even want one, they will certainly benefit from having one, and so will you. At first having two children is so much more exhausting that you will be astounded that you used to complain so much. All parents of two children say the same thing of all parents of one child:

'They don't know they're born.'

(Incidentally, all parents of three children say the same thing of parents of two children.)

Once the youngest is about two, however, life starts to improve. Siblings will play together and with other children more willingly and happily than will only children. I know parents of only children who are still required to keep their charges 'entertained' for vast stretches of the day. Think about it: would you rather play football with your child for four hours, or would you rather watch your two children playing football with each other for four hours while you read a book and sip a mint julep?

And your relationship improves as well. As your children grow, so does your satisfaction in having done all this together and somehow survived it. Each of you realises that this is the only other person in the world who loves your children as much as you do. It counts for a lot.

For second and subsequent births you and your partner will be much better prepared. If she wants to give birth at home in a pool surrounded by 40,000 candles while listening to *Manuel And The Music Of The Mountains*, then why shouldn't she? Meanwhile, you will know whether you want to be there or not. (If there are enough qualified and/or sympathetic womenfolk there, you might be able to wriggle out of it. As Kate Figes writes in *Life*

After Birth: 'Throughout history all cultures that have excluded men from the scene of childbirth have done so because there is little for them actually to do.') I have left this revolutionary and possibly indictable suggestion until the end of the book in the reasonable hope that your partner won't have read this far.

But this is for the future. Right now you have a party to host.

To illustrate how fast the time goes: this will be the first and last birthday party for Junior that will be held primarily for the benefit of the parents. Next year your child will know exactly what's what, will be *au fait* with the concept of 'presents', and won't have to be coerced at gunpoint into blowing out candles on cakes. By the age of two children are very nearly playing with each other, which is to say, seeing something another child is playing with and grabbing it shouting 'Mine! Mine!' But at one, they are only dimly aware of other children, who are not really their friends yet, but the children of friends of their parents, which will never be the same thing, as I'm sure you remember. At a first birthday party the kids wander around intrigued by the novelty of it all, while the parents chat away merrily and get a bit drunk. You'll love it.

Take a look at the other parents and their children. Even if you disregard similarities of height and weight and colouring and all that genetic guff, you may notice certain likenesses between them. For instance, a small girl may already have a similar hairstyle to her mother, or a small boy may have the same slightly pompous mannerisms as his father. We all assume our children will be like us, which is usually an assumption too far, as they are themselves right from the start. But it's around the first birthday that you can begin to see the effects of twelve months of nurture. First babies learn everything from their parents. (Second and subsequent babies learn more from their older siblings, but it all comes back to you in the end.) Oliver James, in his very fine book *They F*** You Up*, describes in gruelling detail how quickly and comprehensively parents can screw up their children, but even if you haven't turned your infant into a schizophrenic you will already have had an enormous influence on the adult he or she will become. James says that most of the crucial work is already done in a year, although you probably can't see it yet. Nevertheless, you can begin to see it in other people and their children, if you look for it. Worse, they can begin to see it in you.

Whoa there. Is this Judgement Day? Will all your wrongdoings be brought to account? Junior may have acquired some of your strange little habits, but that doesn't necessarily point to a future of vagrancy and heroin addiction. This is why the theory of Good Enough Parenting is so comforting and popular. This accepts that nobody is perfect and, moreover, that nobody would want to be, because the 'perfect' parent who got everything right would be a pain in the arse. Far better to be Good Enough, to acknowledge that you are a flawed human being who is going to cock things up from time to time, and if you are happy with that you can get on with the job of parenting without passing on all your anxieties to your children. I think I know in my heart that I am Good Enough.

In the mirror, though, I see Mr Bad Example. I see someone incorrigibly lazy, self-indulgent, quietly manipulative and in bad need of a shave. I see someone who can love his children to distraction – indeed, believes that they are the best thing that ever happened to him – while constantly thinking up new ways to get out of the house. Every evening, during the stressfest that is dinner-bath-bedtime, I fantasise about sitting in a pub quietly with a drink and a book. (When the family go away without me, that's what I do between 6.00 and 7.30 of an evening. Then I come back home, watch the telly by myself, go to bed early, sleep like a breezeblock. For a single man this sort of evening would make you want to top yourself. For me, it is the purest bliss.)

I swear too much. I shout too much. Worse, I go from not shouting at all and talking in a very soft voice though an invisible fury barrier to shouting like a red-faced loon. All the books tell you that this is Very Bad Parenting Indeed.

I eat appallingly. (This paragraph has been prepared with the enthusiastic participation of Mrs Bad Example.) I don't go much on green vegetables and I adore refined sugars, especially whatever it is they put in Mars bars. And Mars bar ice cream. I am prone to defer to Mrs Bad Example on domestic matters, which (she tells me) is a disgraceful example to my son, who will grow up believing that only women cook proper meals. And I am unusually impractical in traditional male ways as well, being inept at all forms of DIY and liable, when things go wrong, to 'run around in circles like a headless chicken until someone else sorts it all out'. (At this point she paused, poured another large glass of red wine and then continued her list of my inadequacies, which I pretended both to listen to and to write down.) I'm sure you could produce an equally illuminating and humiliating list about yourself. But who gives a monkeys? As your child's first birthday party rages, as small children crawl and stagger around your house screaming and crying, as all the mums sit around eating cake and all the dads get quietly drunk, you know that you are at least good enough as a dad, and better than many, and that that's all that matters. You might almost say that all is for the best in the best of possible worlds, if some small person had not just come over to you and vomited on your trousers.

bibliography

There are thousands of books about parenthood, and most are about motherhood. You will probably notice them turning up in your household in the early phases of pregnancy. Many are big and bright and pastel, with lots of photos of chuckling babies and slightly worrying diagrams. Men don't often read these books, but then they are not *for* men as such. Only while researching this book have I finally read some of them, thus becoming a sort of expert after the event. (During the actual pregnancies, of course, I was clueless.) One day I was on the London Underground reading Rachel Cusk's *A Life's Work: On Becoming A Mother*, and taking notes. The man next to me was reading a book as well. I looked over and read the following sentence: 'The helicopter roared overhead.' Nothing better illustrates the gulf between male and female reading habits, although I hope that this book will straddle them to some extent.

The following is a list of some of the more interesting and useful books I have encountered in the researching of this book. Particularly recommended are the Cusk (which is as gloomy a book on motherhood as you could ever hope to read, and also very funny), Desmond Morris's *Babywatching* for the anthropological angle, and Nigel Planer's *A Good Enough Dad,* which is now out of print but occasionally crops up in well-stocked libraries. But all these books have their merits, other than Gina Ford's.

Cohen, David, *The Father's Book* (John Wiley & Sons, 2001).

Cooke, Kaz, *The Rough Guide to Pregnancy and Birth* (Rough Guide/Penguin, 2001).

Cusk, Rachel, *A Life's Work: On Becoming A Mother* (Fourth Estate, 2001).

Figes, Kate, *Life After Birth* (Penguin, 1998).

Ford, Gina, *The New Contented Little Baby Book* (Vermilion, 2002).

Green, Dr Christopher, *Babies!* (Simon & Schuster, 1998).

Hartston, Bill, & Dawson, Jill, *The Ultimate Irrelevant Encyclopædia* (George Allen & Unwin, 1984).

Hogg, Tracy, with Blau, Melinda, *Secrets Of The Baby Whisperer* (Vermilion, 2001).

Macfarlane, Alison, & Mugford, Miranda, *Birthcounts: Statistics Of Pregnancy And Childbirth* (HMSO, 2000).

Morris, Desmond, *Babywatching* (Jonathan Cape, 1991).

Planer, Nigel, *A Good Enough Dad* (Arrow, 1992).

Purves, Libby, *How Not To Be A Perfect Mother* (Harper Collins, 1986).

Rodgers, Gavin, *You're Pregnant Too, Mate!* (Robson Books, 1999).

Sansom, Ian, *The Truth About Babies* (Granta, 2002).

Stoppard, Miriam, *The New Parent* (Dorling Kindersley, 1998).

Symons, Mitchell, *That Book* (Bantam Press, 2003).

Trowell, Judith, & Etchegoyan, Alicia (ed.), *The Importance Of Fathers: A Psychoanalytic Re-evaluation* (Brunner-Routledge, 2002).

Wallechinsky, David, Wallace, Irving, Wallace, Amy, & Wallace, Sylvia, *The Book Of Lists 2* (Corgi, 1981).

Wolf, Dr Danny, *Getting Your Child To Sleep: A Parents' Guide* (Bellew Publishing, 1991).

acknowledgements

I would like to thank the twelve friends who provided the Fathers' Tales: Mike Barfield, Peter Bently, Patrick Bingham, Tom Holland, Patrick Howarth, David Jaques, Howard McMinn, Nick Newman, Neal Ransome, Andy Robson, Simon Rose and David Taylor; my editor Andrew Goodfellow at Ebury Press; my agent Patrick Walsh at Conville & Walsh; Stephen Arkell, Sarah Bellamy, Jean Berkmann-Barwis, Georgia and Thomas Coops, Lucy Curtin, Imelda Dempsey, Selena and Alan Doggett-Jones, Julia Fortier, Bella Goyarts, Ian Hislop, Sarah Jackson, Andy Leonard, Tricia Lovell, Lucy Maycock, Simon O'Hagan, Alex Ross, Terence Russoff, Rose Smith, Russell Taylor and Ceili Williams for ideas, suggestions and encouragement; and Paula Bingham, Martha Berkmann and James Berkmann for absolutely everything.